KU-719-841

THE FLYING SPRINGBOK

796.333
ST. HELENS COMMUNITY LIBRARY
ACC A93162258
CLASS No

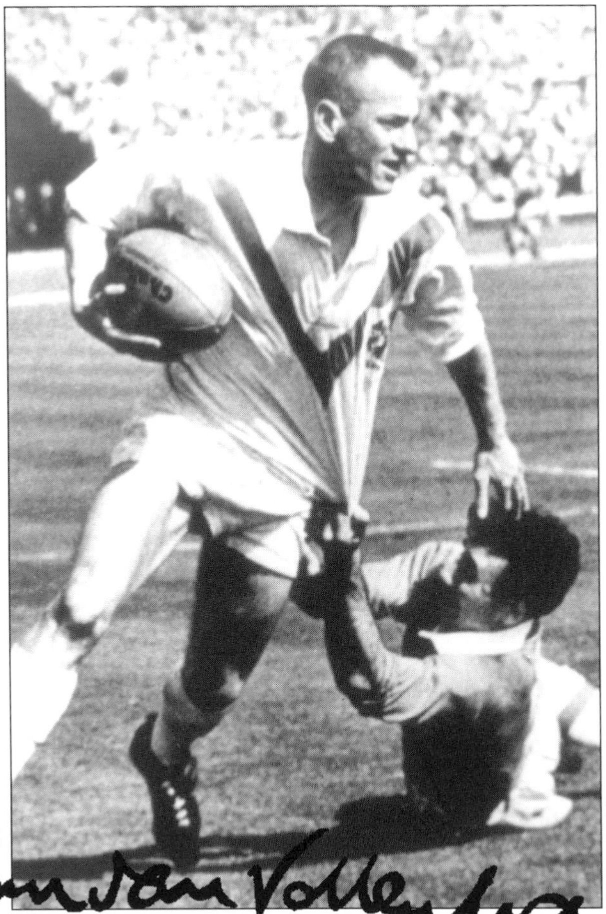

THE RUGBY CAREER OF
TOM VAN VOLLENHOVEN
1955-68

ST. HELENS COMMUNITY LIBRARIES
3 8055 00173 6222

Rugby League's Try of the Century!
Despite his bandaged left thigh, Tom Van Vollenhoven leaves a trail of Hunslet defenders in his wake to score a fantastic touchdown during the 1959 Championship Final at Bradford's Odsal Stadium.

First Published by Alex Service 1993.
© Alex Service. All rights reserved. No part of this publication may be reproduced or transmitted in any form or by any means, electronic or mechanical, including photocopy, recording or any information and retrieval system without permission, in writing, from the publisher.
This book is computer typeset on an
Apple Macintosh IIci System in 10/12pt Garamond.
Designed, computer typeset & printed in Great Britain by Colourplan Design & Print, St.Helens, Merseyside, England.
ISBN 0 9510937 2 X

CONTENTS

Quite simply, this book could not have been written but for the invaluable help of a large number of people. I would, therefore, like to express my sincere gratitude to 'The Team'...

First of all, I would like to thank Tom and Leonie for their help and support, especially during their visit to St.Helens for the Ground Centenary Celebrations in 1990. Yet a project of this nature could not have been attempted without the recollections of Tom's former team-mates at Knowsley Road. Thanks to Ray French, Cen Williams, Alan Briers, Tony Barrow, Steve Llewellyn, Billy Benyon, Dave Markey, Bob Prosser, Joe Robinson, Wilf Smith, Brian McGinn and especially Peter Harvey, for his in-depth analysis of a genius at work! Former Secretary Basil Lowe, Chairman Harry Cook and Coaches Joe Coan and Stan McCormick have also helped to paint a picture of this fantastic winger. The Saints' Past Player's Association and Secretary Geoff Pimblett in particular, have been supportive throughout!

I would like to thank the following players from other Rugby League clubs for their help...Eric Ashton (Wigan), John Stopford (Swinton), Ian Brooke, Keith Holliday and Neil Fox (Wakefield), David Watkins (Salford) and Ken Senior (Huddersfield).

The writings of several well-known rugby scribes have provided me with much inspiration, especially those no longer with us...Tom Ashcroft, Ron Barker and Eddie Waring. I would also like to acknowledge the help of Denis Whittle of the St.Helens Star, Neil Barker of the Wigan Observer...John Huxley...The St.Helens Reporter, The Rugby Leaguer and Open Rugby Magazine.

I should like to express my gratitude to Tony O'Reilly for his magnificent foreword and to Rugby League Historian Robert Gate for his encouragement...and proof reading! Thanks also to the staff of the St.Helens Local History Library; Harold Farrimond for the front cover photograph; Geoff Williams and Saints' modern day 'lensman' Brian Peers; Ernie Day from Warrington, Iris Hunter, Stuart Pyke and the Late Les Charnock. Philip Roberts gave me the spark of inspiration in the early 1980s; Gerry Moore and the Saints' Supporters Club are especially worthy of a mention; Ann Twiss of Rainford, Jeff Butterfield (The Rugby Club, London), Andy Hudson (Rugby League Collector's Club), Curtis Johnstone and Winifred Higham have also played important roles! Thanks to Vernon Roby, the doyen of Rugby League statisticians; Brian Wilson for those sublime Pet Sounds; Trevor Smith from Wigan (at least you had Boston!) and a real Vollenhoven fanatic - Derek Herd - alas no longer with us.

I would like to thank Tony Boal (The 'Grand Master') for his technical expertise and the staff at Colourplan, especially Ian McCue, for making a dream turn into reality! Yet I must also mention my teaching colleagues and the pupils of Broadway Community High School - a real Rugby League 'hotbed' - for their constant encouragement. Last, certainly not least, to my long-suffering wife, Judith and Iain...the next Vollenhoven...or is it Ryan Giggs? We can all dream, can't we! This book is dedicated to everyone who saw the Flying Springbok in full cry...especially Malcom Dunne - a true Saints' fanatic...and an inspiration to us all!

Alex Service

It was May, 1955, on one of those autumnal evenings on the High Veldt....windless, the air crystalline, cigarette smoke hanging in acrid spirals. We were the Young Lions...I, the youngest.....watching a game between Northern Transvaal and Griqualand West and yet to play our first game on South African soil.

It was our first experience as newly-arrived tourists of Rugby Football in South Africa, and it was all so different. An eight panel ball, a brown burnished field, the huge distance the ball travelled at this high altitude of 6,000 feet, and the sheer accelerated pace of every facet of the game on this bone-dry surface.

But the most abiding memory I took away from the game was not of the physical beauty of the surrounds and the enigmatic light, but of a gazelle....a young gazelle....for I had seen for the first time Tom Van Vollenhoven, and it was a sight I shall never forget.

That series changed both our lives. We entered it relatively unknown, and we left five months later on a September evening in Port Elizabeth after a tour marked by it's intensity, it's sportsmanship, it's brilliant rugby but most of all by it's enduring friendships!

Things would never be quite the same for either of us again.

Anthony J.F. O'Reilly.
July 29th.1993

"just like Vollenhoven!"

It was Saturday, 3rd.March, 1990, at Old Trafford. The home of Manchester United had been temporarily commandeered for a blockbusting Rugby League Challenge Cup Semi-Final between the two deadliest rivals in the game-St.Helens and Wigan. Semi-finals, with the twin towers of Wembley 80 minutes away, can be pretty dour affairs. Yet this particular clash had everything-fabulous open rugby, some incredible tackling and a dramatic finish that saw Wigan snatch victory with a controversial try barely two minutes from time! For any afficionado of wing threequarter play, however, the moment to savour came just before half time with the scores tied at 6-6. Saints' hooker Paul Groves picked up from acting half back well inside his own 25 and headed for the left flank. His bullet-like pass cut out centre Paul Loughlin and was collected by left winger Les Quirk on the burst. The Wigan defenders had anticipated a pass to Loughlin and Quirk shot through the gap on the outside, with only full back Hampson barring his way to the line. The 'Cumbrian Flyer' headed for the inside initially, then swerved towards the touchline side, leaving Hampson in his wake as he went over in the corner-75 yards of pure magic that brought the crowd to it's feet. "What a try!" exclaimed the man next to me...."Just like Vollenhoven!" Doubtless Tom himself would have been proud of the effort at such a vital time in the match when the chips were down! The technique was certainly reminiscent of the Great Man, if not quite the scorching pace. Indeed, Vollenhoven remains the yardstick by which wingers...and great individual tries.....are judged by supporters of St.Helens Rugby League Club.

There have been some fine wingers since-Frank Wilson, Les Jones, Roy Mathias, Les Quirk, Alan Hunte, Anthony Sullivan and the man with superb natural talent, who did not quite live up to his enormous potential-Barrie Ledger. Yet in the eyes of those who saw him, there is only one 'Vol.' In the early sixties he was simply the best-in an era when competition on the flanks was intense-with great names such as Stopford, Boston, Bevan...the Australian Ken Irvine...and many more! Although 'The Flying Springbok' is an attempt to re-create those heady days, it also chronicles how the game of Rugby League itself changed over the 'Vollenhoven Decade'.....some say it has never been the same since!

Alex Service,
St.Helens. August 1993.

from sickly youngster to springbok!

WRAPPED IN COTTON WOOL

It seems rather appropriate that Karel Thomas Van Vollenhoven, a man with such tremendous God-given sporting talents, should have been born in a town called Bethlehem, in South Africa's Orange Free State, on April 29th., 1935. Situated north west of the Drakensburg mountains on the High Veld, over 5,000 feet above sea level, Bethlehem is a railway junction at the centre of an important cattle farming and maize growing area. The population of around 20,000 are, like Tom himself, of Dutch origin and speak mostly Afrikaans, a dialect of the Dutch language. Like South Africa as a whole, the community shares an abiding passion for the game of Rugby Union football.

Tom, whose father worked on the railways as an engine driver - he drove the Royal train when the King and Queen visited South Africa in 1947 - was the second youngest of a family of four brothers and a sister. Sport played an important part in the Vollenhoven household. Carl, the eldest son, once held the Orange Free State Lightweight Wrestling Championship and played junior rugby in Bethlehem with his brother Pieter. Sister Carry, the eldest, took a keen interest in sport, unlike brother Andre, the 'baby' of the family. Yet there was also little indication of Tom's future sporting prowess as a youngster. He suffered from a weak chest which needed special protection from the cool, dry climate of that part of the country. *"I had to wear specially-knitted red flannel vests to keep me warm,"* he recalls. *"Even in Summer, my chest closed up when I went outside. I was never allowed to play in the rain or water, that type of thing. I was literally wrapped up in cotton wool! I suppose people felt sorry for me in those days, because I didn't know what it was like to join in games with other boys. Although I didn't feel sorry for myself, I was rather envious when my pals went off to play football or cricket...leaving me as a spectator!"*

The turning point in Tom's life came at the age of nine. His elder brother Carl, a strong, well-built lad caught the eye of a local P.T. Instructor, who considered him an ideal specimen to help with the human pyramid that the boys from the class were learning to form. The Instructor came to the Vollenhoven home to ask if Carl could join the class on a regular basis. It suddenly dawned on young Tom that he was missing out on a whole lot of fun with his weak chest. He promptly burst into tears and almost demanded to join the class with his elder brother. Tom's father allowed him to go, although the family were somewhat resigned to the fact that if there was any bad reaction to the exercises, he would soon pack it in!

The Instructor let Tom off lightly at first, but it gradually became apparent that the exercises were proving extremely beneficial! Two years after joining the class, the disability which doctors had said would prevent him from participating in sport had cleared up completely! Tom became an expert tumbler and took part in gymnastic exhibitions with the class around the Bethlehem area. The metamorphosis from weakling into a fine all-round athlete was only just beginning!

The Original Flying Policeman! Tom in his South African Police Representative jersey.

SCHOOL DAYS

Tom played his first game of rugby at junior school aged eleven. He was developing into quite a sturdy youngster and was soon put in the twelve age group team. His lack of speed meant that he began his rugby career in the forwards! Yet Tom found that beating an opponent with a side-step came naturally to him. Games Masters started to talk of his 'football brain' which more than made up for his overall lack of pace. Still rather ponderous and with little acceleration, Tom was promoted to the school 'B' team and later established himself in the 'A' team. There was little sign of the devastating pace that was to come, however!

At fourteen years of age, Tom moved to the local Voortrekker High School. During the cricket season-from September to March in South Africa-he had developed into a useful medium-paced bowler. Yet after three seasons of rugby, he was still a medium-paced runner! It was by accident that Tom discovered his ability as a sprinter. During his last term at Voortrekker his speed had begun to increase slightly, but he was never considered to be above average. His athletic future seemed to lie in long-distance running and he trained hard for the one and three mile events. One day, at a training session, a friend challenged him-almost jokingly-to a 100 yards sprint. To Tom's great surprise, he pushed his rival all the way and it was not long before he was clocking an amazing 10.5 seconds over the same distance! In Tom's last School Sports, he won the 220 yards sprint with consummate ease-something that had seemed out of the question as he plodded with the forwards not too long before!

Those extra yards certainly did Tom's rugby career no harm whatsoever. While still at school, he gained representative honours, playing in three matches for the Orange Free State Under 19s. as a centre. There was no danger of being pushed back into the pack now! In the close season, Tom also represented the State Under 19s. in athletics over 440 yards.

THE FLYING POLICEMAN

In 1952, at the age of 17, Tom left school to join the South African Police. New recruits trained at the Police College in Pretoria, the administrative capital of the Transvaal, 200 miles from his home in Bethlehem. Following their basic training, recruits were posted throughout South Africa. Apparently Tom had no urge to travel and applied to be posted back to Bethlehem. The request was given the appropriate sympathetic consideration and Vol. found himself in....Pretoria, where, as a Constable, he worked as a Junior Accountant in the Police Paymasters' Office.

When Tom joined the Force, he knew that it would be good for his rugby career. There were some really strong Police teams around at the time, with the Pretoria Police XV acknowledged as one of the strongest. Much of the credit for the success of the side went to the Coach, Sergeant Lucas Strachan, a tough-as-teak former international forward of the 1930s. Under Strachan's supervision, Tom's burning ambition of playing in the First Team was realised less than twelve months after joining the Force-and much more besides! *"I suppose I went to the Police College with a bit of a reputation,"* he recalls. *"I began in the Police Under 19s. side and fortunately was considered good enough to be selected for the Northern Transvaal Under 19s.-which did not just include those from the Police, but the Province as a whole! The experience of representative football helped my selection for the Pretoria Police First XV. It was a fine team and we won the First Division Cup several times. In 1953 came my biggest honour to date when I was selected for Northern Transvaal. I played against the visiting Wallabies-my first taste of playing against an international side."*

As a result of his appearances for Northern Transvaal, Tom was, at 5ft. 10ins. and 12 stones, gaining a reputation as a pacy and deceptively strong centre threequarter. Yet he was very much the all-round sportsman by this time. He also played hockey, for the Old Students' Club in Pretoria as a centre forward-and had trials for Northern Transvaal-but rugby was his number one priority! During the Summer months, however, he was able to indulge in his passion for athletics-once again with considerable success.

Unfortunately, Tom was unable to gain selection for the Police team because of a senior colleague called Gideon Van Heerden. During Vol's first two years in the Force, Van Heerden's superior pace had given him international recognition. In the face of such competition, Tom had to turn to other branches of athletics to represent the Police. He enjoyed some success as a long-jumper and partnered Van Heerden in the relay team. While representing Northern Transvaal, he jumped 24ft. 5inches, yet his chance to represent Pretoria Police as a sprinter came rather unexpectedly at the age of nineteen. Van Heerden suffered a muscle injury. Tom took his place in the team and took part in the 1955 South African Police Championships at Pretoria. It was one of his greatest sporting achievements to win the 100 yards final in 9.8 seconds-

equalling the Pretoria Police record into the bargain!

In December 1955, a German athletics team visited South Africa. By this time, Van Heerden was fully fit and running for South Africa once more. Despite this, both men were included in the Police team. Although Tom was still interested in the long jump, he concentrated on the 100 yards. When running for Northern Transvaal against the Germans, he showed what devastating pace he had now acquired by winning in the impressive time of 9.8 seconds. Little wonder, that on December 10th., 1955, the Northern Transvaal relay team-Tom, Van Heerden, Petty and Holland-set up a new Empire and Commonwealth record of 41.1 seconds for the 440 yards relay. Ironically, Van Heerden never exceeded 9.9 for the hundred yards in police events. His fastest time for his country, however, was 9.6!

THE STUFF DREAMS ARE MADE OF!

Every rugby fan in South Africa looked forward to the 1955 season and the mouth-watering prospect of four Test Matches against the visiting British Lions, especially since the 1951/52 Springbok Machine had mowed it's way through Britain and France losing only one of 31 matches! The newly arrived Lions saw Northern Transvaal hand out a 15-9 beating to the Western Province at Loftus Versfeld on June 15th. The British squad had been particularly impressed by the power play of the Northern Transvaal pack. Yet one man who definitely caught the eye was a close-cropped threequarter called Van Vollenhoven, playing on the right wing, who had tormented the opposition every time he received the ball! Needless to say, Tom's name came to the notice of the National Selectors and he took part in the Test Trials held in late July. He made quite an impact. To his great surprise....and obvious delight, Tom was selected to play in the First Test in his more accustomed left centre position. He was, at 20, the youngest member of the side and one of nine new caps. Bethlehem's first-ever Springbok had come a long way from those early days as a sickly youngster, when a sporting career had looked totally out of the question!

Electric Youth!
Tom in try scoring action for Northern Transvaal versus Western Province, July 1954.
(Pretoria News)

CHAPTER TWO

Tom the Lion tamer!

A RUDE AWAKENING

The British Lions' tour was capturing the imagination of rugby-crazy South Africa in a big way. Captained by the Irish lock forward Robin Thompson, who later joined Warrington Rugby League Club, the side won ten of their first twelve matches, scoring 248 points against 103. The Lions were particularly strong in the centres, with the English pairing of Jeff Butterfield and Phil Davies posing a distinct threat, while at fly-half, the Welsh Wizard Cliff Morgan was always adept at making the initial break and getting his backs moving. One man who had really become a crowd favourite, especially with the 'bobby-soxers' was the red-haired Irish winger Tony O'Reilly. The 19 year old made try-scoring look easy with his great strength and speed.

There was, therefore, much excitement before the First Test at Ellis Park, Johannesburg-a match everyone wanted to see! A crowd of 9,000 waited at Ellis Park to buy tickets on the Monday before the game. 3,000 had waited at the ground over the weekend, taking their places in the queue straight after the tourists had beaten Transvaal by 36-13 at the same venue on the Saturday. There was a thriving black market in tickets, with two guinea tickets selling for over 12. Before the kick off, on 6th.August, 1955, there were over 90,000 packed into the stadium-a world record for a Rugby Union game.

Tom's partner in the new-look South African line-up was Theunis Briers, a pacy winger from Western Province, who was almost omitted from the final Springbok trial in which he forced his way into the side! It was to be an afternoon of mixed fortunes for the left-wing pairing. The Lions struck the first blow when Irish winger Pedlow scored an unconverted try in the corner, despite Briers' attempt to push him over the touchline. South Africa drew level with two penalties from full back Van Der Schiff and the game swung their way dramatically in the 35th. minute when Briers scored as a result of a tremendous blind side move instigated by scrum half Tommy Gentles. Although Van Der Schiff converted, the Lions struck back a minute later. Morgan sped past his opposite number Clive Ulyate and fed Butterfield. The home threequarter line, including his opposite number, Vollenhoven, streamed across in anticipation of a link up with O'Reilly. Yet the classy centre swung inside with great panache to score a converted try under the posts to reduce the deficit to 8-11 at the interval.

At the start of the second half, the Lions lost forward Reg Higgins with a twisted knee. No momentum was lost, however, as Cliff Morgan proceeded to turn the match with a brilliant solo effort from a scrum in the 43rd.minute, which Cameron gleefully converted. To the horror of the huge crowd, South Africa conceded two further tries, from Greenwood and O'Reilly-both a result of full back Van Der Schiff's inability to deal with seemingly innocuous kicks. Cameron added the points on both occasions to cap a fine spell of 15 points in ten minutes. The 14-man Lions seemed in total control at 23-11. Yet in the 61st.minute right winger Swart pulled a try back for the Union as the visiting forwards began to tire rapidly. Virtually at the end of normal time the powerful forward Chris Koch smashed his way over for Van Der Schiff to convert. In the two and a half minutes of injury time left, Retief, Fry and Sinclair handled for Briers to break past two tacklers and touch down 12 yards in from the flag. At 22-23 it all hung on Van Der Schiff's conversion. Unfortunately, the full back pulled his kick badly and hung his head in anguish long before the ball even reached the posts! South Africa had been beaten for the first time in the opening Test of a Home International series since 1896. It was also the highest score ever recorded against the Springboks in 64 years of international rugby!

The fact that the Lions were considered to be the finest attacking combination ever to visit South Africa was of little consolation to the Springboks-and Tom Vollenhoven in particular. The knives were out with a vengeance! One critic, Philip Nel, the 1937 Springbok Captain, highlighted the '"shoddy tackling of the inside men, responsible for every one of the Lions' scoring movements." Tom faced an anxious wait for the announcement of the Second Test team and was hardly optimistic of keeping his place!

A GLORIOUS REPRIEVE!

Tom could not bear to listen to the radio on the evening that the team was announced and went to the cinema with his Fiancee Leonie Lawrence instead. As they were leaving at the end of the show, the names of the South African XV were flashed onto the screen. To his great relief, the selectors had retained Tom in the side, although they had moved him out to the left wing and brought in Wilf Rosenberg from the Transvaal as his centre. Like Tom in later years, Rosenberg, the 'Flying Dentist' would also play Rugby League football in England, with Leeds and Hull. Theunis Briers switched to the right, where he was partnered by Sinclair. Roy Dryburgh, of Natal replaced the unfortunate Van Der Schiff at full back.

As he took up his position in front of a 46,000 crowd at Newlands, Cape Town, Tom knew that his Springbok career was in the balance. His most important task was to subdue the attacking threat of the Lions' flyer Tony O'Reilly on the opposite flank-no mean feat! It was the Lions who went ahead in the 18th.minute when Scottish full back Cameron successfully kicked a 25 yard penalty goal. The home forwards, ably led by Skipper and second rower Stephen Fry hammered away at the Lions, seemingly to no avail. At last, in the 37th. minute came the breakthrough the vociferous crowd had been waiting for. Retief and Fry drove forward before handing on to Sinclair, who cross-kicked. Yet it was too strong for his forwards and threatened to put his side in danger. There were three Lions, Davies, O'Reilly and Cameron, under the ball against Vollenhoven, with the field wide open for a British counter attack. Yet with a great leap-more reminiscent of an Australian Rules footballer-Tom plucked the ball out of the air and sped 25 yards to the line. Unfortunately Dryburgh was unable to capitalise on this magnificent piece of opportunism and the scores remained at 3-3 until the interval.

South Africa 25 British Lions 9, Second Test, Newlands, August 20th 1955. Tom Van Vollenhoven crashes over for his second try of the match...and there was one more to come! Centre partner Wilf Rosenberg (with the left knee bandaged) is about to acclaim a great touchdown.

THE HAT TRICK KING!

In the 46th.minute, the Lions' defence cracked once more. This time it was fly half Ulyate who was the initiator. His well-placed grubber kick was snapped up by Sinclair, who drew full back Cameron before feeding Vollenhoven. Despite a last-ditch tackle from Greenwood, Tom crashed over in the corner for his second try, which Dryburgh failed to convert. Such was the Springbok dominance, that Tony O'Reilly had few genuine running chances. Four minutes later, the genius of Tom Van Vollenhoven would add considerably to the big Irishman's personal nightmare! He received a pass from Tommy Gentles 45 yards out near the touchline, before beating O'Reilly on the inside. Opposing scrum half Jeeps was totally outpaced as Tom bore down on full back Cameron. The Scot was left standing with a superb feint and inside swerve, as Tom went on to plant the ball between the posts-one of the greatest moments in South African rugby history!

The Springbok forwards were well on top at this stage, providing the backs with further running chances. Rosenberg scorched in for try number four and provided full back Dryburgh with a fifth, which he converted for a 17-3 lead, ruling out any possibility of a Lions' revival. South Africa increased their lead still further, when Briers roared in for a sixth touchdown. A total rout was avoided, however, when Butterfield took Morgan's reverse pass for a classic score. To cap a feast of attacking rugby, each side crossed the line in the last four minutes, leaving the Springboks winners by a resounding 25-9 margin that would have been higher but for poor place-kicking!

Although praise was heaped on the South African forwards for a powerful display, the headlines were full of the part played by the 20 year old 'Flying Policeman' from Pretoria! Tom's feat of scoring three tries in a row for the Springboks was unique in a home Test Match, although it had been equalled several times and surpassed on tour. Indeed, no player had previously scored three tries-consecutively or otherwise-in any Test in South Africa! "It must be said that we saw very little of the ball that day," remembers the former British Lion's centre Jeff Butterfield-proprietor of the world-famous 'Rugby Bar' in London. "Mind you, it was a case of wing threequarter brilliance from Vollenhoven. He had three chances....and took them superbly! As wingers go, I have certainly seen nobody better than him-he was like lightening!" Vol's memorable performance guaranteed him a place in the remaining internationals-and the vital Third Test in Pretoria on September 3rd. which the South Africans hoped to win to go one up in the rubber.

SOUTH AFRICA 25
BRITISH LIONS 9
SECOND TEST,
NEWLANDS (CAPE TOWN)
AUGUST 20TH.1955

SOUTH AFRICA
Dryburgh (2 conversions, try); Briers (try), Sinclair, Rosenberg (try), Van Vollenhoven (3 tries); Ulyate, Gentles; Bekker, Van Der Merwe, Koch, Fry (Capt.), Du Rand, Claassen, Ackermann (try), Retief.

BRITISH LIONS
Cameron (penalty goal); O'Reilly, Butterfield (try), Davies, Griffiths; Morgan, Jeeps; W.Williams, B.Meredith (try), C.Meredith, Greenwood, R.Thompson (Capt.), R.Williams, Robins, Reid.

Referee-M.Slabber

Attendance-46,000

ROARING BACK!

Located some 900 miles to the North East of Cape Town, the Lions were faced with much hotter, drier weather in Pretoria-not to mention an altitude difference of more than 5,000 feet! Yet they had time to acclimatize themselves for a fortnight before the Test with successes against Eastern and Northern Transvaal-the latter a 14-11 victory despite a fine opportunist try from adopted local boy Tom Van Vollenhoven. Indeed, the threat of Vol. forced the Lions' Management to switch Tony O'Reilly over to the left wing, leaving Welshman Gareth Griffiths to cope with the new Springbok sensation.
Unlike the tremendous open rugby at Newlands, the Third Test soon developed into a dour struggle characterised by much safety-first kicking and no less than 65 line-outs during the eighty minutes! Yet it was an open secret that Lions' Skipper, Cliff Morgan, took the field with a 'win at all costs' dictum from the Management. The high stakes meant a reluctance to open out play and take risks of any sort. The Lions took the lead just before half time with a left foot drop by Butterfield-the first of it's kind in 363 points on tour! In the 52nd.minute, Lions' full back Baker kicked a thirty yard penalty. Dryburgh replied with a 50 yard penalty dropped goal shortly after, to raise Springbok hopes. Yet on the hour, Butterfield's crucial try clinched victory for the Lions, despite a further Dryburgh penalty shortly after.

The Lions fully deserved their 9-6 success. Indeed, the margin of victory tended to flatter the home side. It was suggested that five of the Springbok pack were from the

Springboks Triumphant!
South Africa's successful line up against the British Lions, Second Test 1955. Back Row: J. Claassen, D. Ackerman, D. Retief. Middle Row: W. Rosenberg, H. Becker, R. Dryburgh, A. Koch, T. Briers, A. Van Der Merwe. Second Row: J. Du Rand (v.Capt), Mr. M. Louw (Manager), S. Fry (Capt), Dr. D. Craven (Coach), D. Sinclair. Front Row: C. Ulyate, T. Gentles, K.T. Van Vollenhoven.

coast and had too short a time to get used to the hotter, drier conditions! According to A.C.Parker in 'Giants of South African Rugby': "Briers and Vollenhoven did not help matters by throwing in crookedly at the line-outs, which meant more scrummaging for an already tired lot of forwards." Both sets of wingers found themselves starved of possession: "Vollenhoven, the Second Test hero, did put in a couple of good runs, but each time he had to forage for the ball. For that matter, Griffiths and O'Reilly saw little of the ball."

South Africa was in danger of losing a home international series for the first time in 59 years. There was a return to the lower altitude of Port Elizabeth for the Final Test, however, where the Springboks had won their last five Test Matches on the Crusader Ground.

HONOURS EVEN

The Lions were coming to the end of an exhausting tour in which they had travelled over 9,000 miles and were, perhaps, losing that vital 'edge.' Fly half Cliff Morgan played in the Final Test with knee ligament damage. The little Welsh Master would not be the potent attacking force he had been in the previous matches. Good quality ball for the wingers seemed to be at a premium once again, as the South African forwards kept the ball tight in the first half in an effort to wear down their opponents. Yet it was the Lions who scored first with a try from prop forward Greenwood in the 13th.minute converted by Pedlow. The Springboks came under severe pressure for most of the first half, but with a minute to go before the interval, fly half Clive Ulyate cross-kicked initially for Briers. Full back Pedlow looked to have the kick covered, but let the ball slip out of his hands for Briers to touch down.

Amazingly, two minutes after half time, another kick by Ulyate was fumbled by Pedlow for Briers to take advantage once more! At 6-5 the Springbok pack began to bring the Lions into submission. A try by Ulyate, converted by Dryburgh increased South Africa's lead still further. Then came the moment that brought the 37,000 crowd to their feet! A heel against the head saw Ulyate streak round the blind side to feed Vollenhoven, who after outpacing his opposite number Griffiths, beat full back Baker with a magical inside swerve to score a crucial try.

A dropped goal by Ulyate put South Africa into an unassailable 17-5 lead. Although the lions replied with a try by Tony O'Reilly-which cost him a dislocated shoulder-Retief added to the home side's total with a further try, converted by Dryburgh. After the final whistle, the Springboks were mobbed by a wildly enthusiastic crowd eager to celebrate the squaring of the series against arguably the greatest side ever to tour South Africa!

CHAPTER THREE

Making the break

SOWING THE SEEDS OF LEAGUE

Tom's home town of Bethlehem gave him a fine welcome after the Fourth Test. As the first-ever Springbok from the town, he was a special guest of honour at a dance at the Railway Institute. To mark the occasion, he presented his coveted green and gold Springbok jersey to Voortrekker High School. Despite enjoying such a tremendous series against the Lions, however, Tom hoped to fulfill another ambition by being selected for the tour of Australia and New Zealand, to leave the Union in May, 1956.

Although Tom had achieved international acclaim as a left winger, he continued to play as a centre for the Pretoria Police. He was earmarked as one of the 100 players to take part in three trials during April to select a squad of 30 to make the trip. In the first trial, held at Cape Town, Tom's dream looked to be in tatters. Playing on the left wing, he chased a loose ball when an opponent crashed into him. The result-a badly bruised thigh muscle. Unfit for the remainder of the trials, Tom was concerned that he might be overlooked by the selectors. Fortunately, he was chosen on the basis of his form against the Lions.

South Africa won all their six matches in Australia. Although Tom played in the two Test Matches, both were dour, forward-orientated affairs, with few genuine scoring chances. He did manage to get on the scoresheet in the Second Test, courtesy of a dropped goal-only the second time that he had ever attempted one! Against New South Wales at the famous Sydney Cricket ground, however, he showed his tremendous finishing ability with two fine tries, the second from just inside his own half after he had picked up a loose ball. Before the squad left for the main part of the tour to New Zealand, they were taken to see the Rugby League clash between New South Wales and Queensland, also at the S.C.G. Tom liked what he saw, a game in which a winger could really show his paces. Yet the professional code was taboo in South Africa and Tom decided to keep his views to himself. As he recalls: *"We were very much influenced by the Tour Manager, Dr.Danie Craven-one of the major figures in the game back home. We were just so proud to be representing our country. To be honest, I hadn't even remotely considered the possibility of playing League at the time!"*

The second leg of the tour was a much more difficult proposition-beating the visiting Springboks had become a national obsession in rugby-mad New Zealand! Like all the Springboks, Tom was feted wherever he went...almost like royalty! His close-cropped hairstyle made him extremely distinctive and youngsters soon began to sport similar 'crew-cuts' in his honour! The home side won three out of the four Test matches-New Zealand's first win over South Africa in sixty years. As a result of injury and loss of form, Tom played in only one of the Tests, at Lancaster Park, Christchurch. Forming a left wing partnership with room-mate Wilf Rosenberg, Tom helped to set up a try for flank forward 'Butch' Lochner early in the second half. Yet they found the half time deficit of 11 points an impossible hurdle to overcome. Making his debut for New Zealand that day was full back Don 'The Boot' Clarke, who became a legendary figure on the international front in later years. In the early 1960s, Don was approached by the St.Helens Rugby League Club, but never ' turned.'

On Christmas Eve, 1956, Tom became engaged to Miss Leonie Lawrence, left the South African Police and went to work in a copper mine in Northern Rhodesia, supervising underground workers. Yet there was another important meeting that was to change his life before he left Pretoria. The Late George Duckworth, the former Lancashire and England wicket-keeper, was Scorer and Baggage Master with the M.C.C. Cricket XI who played in Pretoria in December. George was a Director of Warrington Rugby League Club at the time and it was at his invitation that Tom went to see him in a Pretoria Hotel. Tom was told what rugby league was all about and that Warrington were showing an interest. Not once did Duckworth suggest that he should actually sign for Warrington, however, indicating that the Lancashire club's interest was no more than lukewarm!

DOUBLE YOUR MONEY!

According to Tom, Northern Rhodesia-or Zambia as it is now-was a very rich country. *"It certainly was good money out there,"* he recal ls. *"There was an incentive called the 'Copper Bonus'.......at one stage it was 100% of your salary. If you earned £1,000, your bonus was £1,000-you could double your money! We worked 12 hour shifts, from six in the morning to six at night and played our club rugby mostly on Sundays. We always had great parties after the matches-a good social scene!"* Based in Chingola, Tom played for the Nchanga club. The team went on a short tour during the Easter of 1957 without their star Springbok threequarter. Yet Tom had more important matters to attend to, having returned to South Africa to marry his fiancee, Leonie Lawrence, on Easter Saturday. The happy couple flew back to Chingola on the Monday for Tom to resume work the following day!

While living in Chingola, he was still involved with representative rugby, being selected for Northern Rhodesia, including matches for the famous Currie Cup. As Tom and Leonie settled down to married life, there was further interest from English Rugby League. In June 1956, a letter arrived from Wigan, who were prepared to offer a sum of £2,000 for his signature. *"I told Leonie to throw it away,"* he recalls, *"I simply wasn't interested."* Yet Tom was persuaded by his wife to reply if only to find out more. Indeed, Wigan indicated that they would be sending a representative over to Chingola to interview him. By early September, however, St.Helens were showing more than a passing interest. The chase for Vollenhoven's signature was developing into an intriguing head-to-head clash between two of the oldest-and deadliest-rivals in Rugby League!

OUR MAN IN SALISBURY

During the chase to sign Vollenhoven, the St.Helens club had an ace up their sleeve. His name was Ted Higham, ironically Wigan-born and bred, a schoolmaster at

Saints 'Man in Salisbury'.
Ted Higham - a Wiganer by birth - who played such a crucial role in bringing Tom Van Vollenhoven to St.Helens. Higham wrote a successful coaching book during his time in Rhodesia - 'High Speed Rugby' much acclaimed by the critics.
(Mrs. W. Higham)

St.George's College in Salisbury (Now Harare) Southern Rhodesia. Higham had played rugby league for Warrington and was a good friend of the St.Helens Coach Jim Sullivan. The club's initial offer was sent to Higham, who was seen to be the first point of contact with Vollenhoven. A letter from Higham to Jim Sullivan, dated 20th.September 1957, confirmed the first stage in the quest for the Flying Springbok:

"Dear Jim,
Received your wire today. Vollenhoven lives in the Copperbelt-750 miles to the North. I've airmailed the content of your offer plus an explanation, plus an offer of personal advice which is what he may be needing. For a Springbok to go 'pro' is a bigger and weightier step than say, an Aussie, the feeling being what it is in the Union. If he wants advice, I'll do what I can and wire you immediately whatever his decision is. The fall of the copper bonus recently may affect or change earlier decisions-as being a miner he must have been earning between £150-£200 A MONTH!-with the possibilty of other inducements."

Back in Chingola, Tom sought the help of an acquaintance called Lusk-an electrician-who originally hailed from Middlesbrough. *"I told him of the offers from Wigan and St.Helens,"* remembers Tom, *"And he said that they were the two biggest clubs in the Rugby League at the time. He says 'Don't be silly, tell them both you want more money.' So I sent a telegram to both clubs at the same time. Whoever offered the biggest amount, I would accept!"*

Ted Higham, in one of his communications to Jim Sullivan described Vollenhoven as *'A shy, quiet chap, totally unequipped for barter.'* Needless to say, it was Lusk *'A shrewd character who knew the ropes,'* who became Tom's Agent during the negotiations. On October 2nd., Lusk contacted Ted Higham and asked for £4,000 on the player's behalf *'Without quibble, plus the usual endorsements.'* Ted tried, initially, to call his bluff by saying that the figure was too high. Lusk replied that he had written to Wigan that morning. On October 2nd., Higham wired Jim Sullivan with the news that Vollenhoven was prepared to consider terms. A special meeting of the St.Helens Board of Directors was held, under the Chairmanship of Harry Cook, when it was decided that all efforts be made to secure Vollenhoven's signature on professional forms. As former Club Secretary Basil Lowe recalled: *"From the time of that meeting, everyone connected in any way was pledged to the utmost secracy. In fact, the name of the player was not again to be mentioned until the mission had been achieved!"*

On the Board's instructions, Higham sent a telegram to Vollenhoven offering £3,500 to turn professional also asking Tom not to sign for any other club without getting in touch with him first. Several days passed without word from the player. On Saturday, October 5th., a cable was sent by St.Helens authorising Ted to offer £4,000. The final, amazing chapter in the race to sign Tom Van Vollenhoven was revealed in a letter sent by Higham to Jim Sullivan on October 6th:

"Dear Jim,
I received your final cable late in the day as I'd been out all afternoon with a cricket team. I phoned through to cable, but being Saturday, they couldn't promise to have it delivered before Monday morning which could have meant a 50-50 chance with Wigan. This would have naturally made Lusk raise the price and dangle the carrot before two donkeys. I was in a fix. However, a parent of one of the boarders is a District Commissioner in Northern Rhodesia and lived within 30 miles of the player's home in Kabundi. I got the boy to phone his Dad (800 miles away) and I begged him to drive to Vollenhoven's house and asked him to phone me between 8 and 9 last night-and kept my fingers crossed that the D.C. would find him at home. In fact, he drove there to find Tom and his wife leaving for a party-on the point, in fact, of closing the front door-which would have resulted in no phone conversation clinching the deal had he been three or four minutes late. Lusk phoned me at 9pm and Vollenhoven became a Saint. Airfare was saved and time, which was more precious. Wigan's wire arrived on Sunday morning (The day after). This he would have accepted, he has since told me. A Saturday night cable from me would not have arrived until Monday and there was no plane until late Sunday!"

MISSION ACCOMPLISHED

Despite Wigan's identical offer of £4,000 arriving the following day, Tom was true to his word and pledged himself to the St.Helens club. Indeed, the Saints had won the race for the Flying Springbok in some style! The telegram boy delivering Wigan's offer suffered a puncture and was significantly delayed. It is reputed that he was overtaken en route to the Vollenhoven household by the powerful mercedes driven by Ted Higham's 'Special Envoy'-District Commissioner Bentley O.B.E.

Even then, contracts and signing on forms had to be dispatched and signed and transport arranged. Ted Higham continued to play a leading role, in the procedings, however, and Tom and Leonie were flown to Salisbury, where they spent a week at the Hotel Windsor. In a letter to Saints' Chairman Harry Cook, Higham gave three good reasons for such a course of action: *"First-he was on tap to sign the contract. No agreement is worth a jot unless you have a signature; secondly-Wigan's representative might easily have got to him with an extra inducement and a signature; thirdly-he was under considerable amateur pressure, which couldn't have been pleasant."* Although Ted had arranged a tentative air booking to London, plans were thwarted by the need for passport alterations, together with yellow fever innoculations for the couple. These were compulsory for air travellers, as all aircraft refuelled in the part of Africa where the disease was endemic, during the flight to England. *"They don't like kicking their heels about,"* he added, *"And are looking forward to getting away. They seem a rather pleasant couple-rather shy and a little bewildered yet. The news has made a tremendous impression here. He looks very fit!"*

Tom remembers that the Rugby Union establishment-Dr.Craven in particular-were very disappointed:

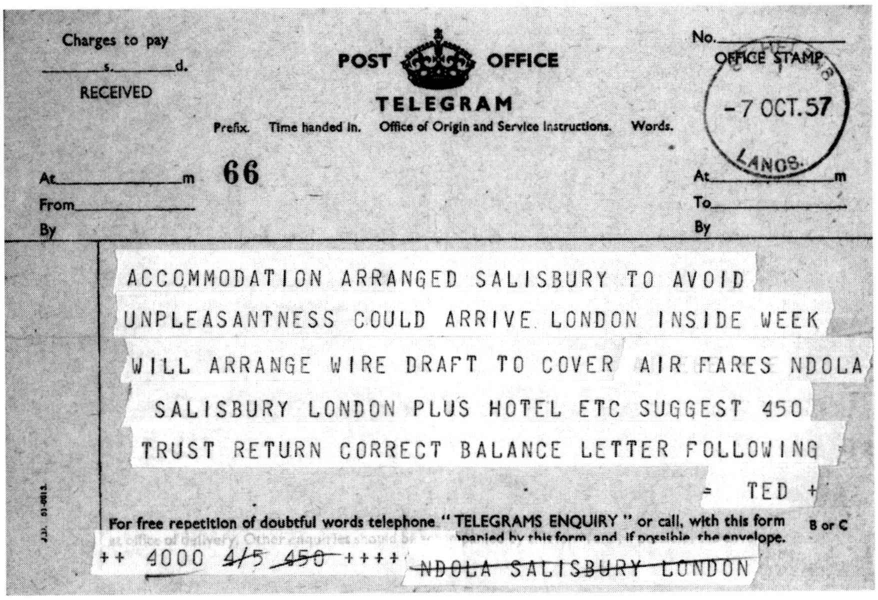
Charges to pay
s. d.
RECEIVED
POST OFFICE
TELEGRAM
Prefix. Time handed in. Office of Origin and Service Instructions. Words.
No.
OFFICE STAMP
-7 OCT.57
At m 66
From
By
At m
To
By
ACCOMMODATION ARRANGED SALISBURY TO AVOID
UNPLEASANTNESS COULD ARRIVE LONDON INSIDE WEEK
WILL ARRANGE WIRE DRAFT TO COVER AIR FARES NDOLA
SALISBURY LONDON PLUS HOTEL ETC SUGGEST 450
TRUST RETURN CORRECT BALANCE LETTER FOLLOWING
= TED +
For free repetition of doubtful words telephone "TELEGRAMS ENQUIRY" or call, with this form ... panied by this form and, if possible, the envelope. B or C
++ 4000 4/5 ~~450~~ ++++ ~~NDOLA SALISBURY LONDON~~

Ted Higham's telegram to the St.Helens club clearly indicates the depth of feeling generated by Tom's proposed switch of codes!

"It was just as well they flew us to Salisbury, because of the commotion it caused...the South African people hear too much propaganda against the professional code to feel kindly towards it. I was made to feel like an outcast. I just had to phone my parents and tell them I was going to England. They weren't too happy about it either!"

It was with some relief that a cable was received at St.Helens' Knowsley Road ground which read: *"Mr. and Mrs. Tom Vollenhoven airborne and arriving London Airport, Flight S.A. 218 on Saturday, 19th.October, midday. Check details and meet party."*

Ted Higham had never known a fortnight quite like it! Apart from the tremendous organisation required, there was also the need for him to keep a low profile, as he taught in a strong rugby union college and obviously did not want to jeopardise his position in any way. The Saints' initiative in utilising such a contact paid handsome dividends. Yet the club and it's supporters owe a debt of gratitude to the Late Ted Higham for his part in turning a 'Flying Springbok' into a 'Saint'!

An Agreement made the

of 195

N.B.— Leave words in single brackets when Club a Company. Use words in double brackets when Club an ordinary Members' Club

BETWEEN BASIL LOWE

(the Secretary of and acting pursuant to Resolution and Authority for behalf of the ST. HELENS RUGBY Football Club L

((~~being two Members of the Committee of the~~ ~~Footbal~~ ~~on behalf of themselves and all other members of the said Club~~)) (herei referred to as "the Club") of the one part and KAREL VON VOLLENHOVE (hereinafter called "the Player") of the other part WHEREBY it is agre follows:—

N.B.— Strike out words in brackets not required

1. In consideration of the stipulations and agreement on the part of the hereinafter contained, the Player hereby agrees with the Club that he will, du the next (or remainder of the present) playing season of the Rugby Foot League, well and faithfully and to the best of his ability and skill, play the gam Rugby League football for the Club, either for their First Team, Second Team as a reserve to either Team, as and when and where he may from time to time called upon by the said Club so to do. The Player shall do everything necess to get and keep himself in the best possible condition so as to render the m efficient service to the Club and will carry out all the training and oth instructions of the Club through its representative officials.

2. The Player agrees to abide by and observe all the Rules of the Club and t obey, observe, and perform all reasonable orders of the Directors, Committee, o the Secretary, Manager, or Trainer of the Club and of the Captain selected by the Club of the Team in which the Player shall from time to time be chosen to play, also to abide by and observe all Rules and Directions or alterations or additional Rules (if any), which may from time to time be made by the Club.

3. The Player shall observe and be subject to all the Rules, Regulations and Bye-laws of the Rugby Football League or any other League Union or Combination of which the Club shall be a member.

N.B.— Strike out words in brackets not required

4. In consideration of the Player faithfully observing and performing the stipulations and agreements herein contained, the Club hereby agree that they will during the (next or present) playing season of the said League pay the Player the salary of NINE POUNDS for each Match played in by the Player which may be won, ~~the sum of~~ ~~for each Match played in by the Player which may be drawn, and~~ the sum of FIVE POUNDS for each Match played in by the Player which may be lost, when playing for the First Team, and the sum of FIVE POUNDS for each Match when acting as Reserve to the First Team, such last mentioned sum to be inclusive of Second Team wages when, although reserve to the First Team, he may be called upon by the Directors or Committee to play with the Second Team. One pound extra to be paid when playing at Whitehaven, Barrow, Workington, or in Yorkshire.

The draft of Karel Von Vollenhoven's (sic) contract with the St.Helens Rugby League Club. Unlike the contract system in today's game, players were payed per match. Notice the extra pound bonus for a win in Cumbria or Yorkshire.

CHAPTER FOUR

Strangers in a strange land

THE SOUTH AFRICAN METEOR!

The Saints' cloak and dagger operation meant that news of the signing was only released as the couple were heading towards London. Needless to say, Tom's defection caused banner headlines in both South Africa and England. Indeed, news of his impending arrival and debut caused a sensation in the glass town of St.Helens: *"Saints have their own meteor,"* proclaimed rugby league correspondent Tom Ashcroft in the St.Helens Reporter-a reference to Russia's recent launching of the world's first satelite. *"Even this has not created more discussion locally than the Saints' harnessing of the South African rugby meteor Tom Van Vollenhoven. While scientists have been tracking the course of the satelite, Saints' officials have been arranging for the flight of the Springbok with a view to launching him against Leeds on October 26th. In the nick of time the club has brought into use a modernised telephone system at Knowsley Road to issue all the information the Rugby League world has demanded of the movements and intentions of South Africa's Sportsman of the Year!"*

Harry Cook, the Saints' Chairman and Secretary Basil Lowe had made an overnight journey to London Airport to greet the couple. *"We still wondered and worried whether the player would be on the plane,"* remembers Basil. *"Actually the flight was late, and we sat rather nervously in the airport lounge snatching at bits of information that came through. At last the plane landed, fortunately containing our new signing and a bevy of photographers rushed to the scene!"*

Tom and Leonie were quite bewildered by the reception, but they were given little pause for thought. Some four hours later they were sat in front of television cameras at the Granada Studios in Manchester after a hectic car dash. Eddie Waring, the famous commentator asked Basil Lowe how much the club's new signing had cost. *"A lot of money!"* came the reply.

The following morning there was a press conference at Knowsley Road, where the official signing took place. Tom recalls that the Saints' Coach Jim Sullivan was a tremendous help during the somewhat daunting prospect of facing the sporting press and media: *"He took to me straight away and went out of his way to help me. At the press conference, he sat next to me. As they fired questions at me....Jim answered every one - he had certainly done his homework!"* Indeed, Tom was more used to speaking his native Afrikaans than English, making communication slightly difficult early on. Yet it was not long before Sullivan was putting Tom through his paces out on the pitch, once again for the benefit of the cameras. There was much to learn about the new code, especially the play-the-ball rule - somewhat alien to a former rugby union player who is used to releasing the ball as soon as he is tackled. Huge crowds lined the training pitch on Tuesday evening to watch the new signing train with his new team-mates. *"If we had charged admission fees for those early training sessions,"* recalls Basil Lowe, *"We could have recouped a large slice of his signing on fee before he had even played a game!"*

New kid in town!
Tom wears the famous red and white jersey of St.Helens for the first time in October 1957.
(St.Helens Reporter)

THE MIDAS TOUCH

Founder members of the breakaway Northern Union in 1895, the Saints had enjoyed only sporadic success before Jim Sullivan joined the club as Coach before the start of the 1952/53 campaign. A magnificent motivator of players, Sullivan coached the Saints to the League Championship at the end of his first season at Knowsley Road. In 1955/56, his team brought the coveted Challenge Cup back to St. Helens for the first time. Always an advocate of the 'power game,' Sullivan relied increasingly upon his big pack of forwards to grind down the opposition in the early weeks of the 1957/58 season. The unspectacular 'creeping barrage' approach certainly won matches, but did not meet with the whole-hearted approval of Saints' supporters, who favoured a more open brand of football-mirrored by a disappointing 9,000 attendance for the home 'derby' clash with Warrington on September 28th.
On the flanks, the Saints could call on Frank Carlton, a local lad who had scored a memorable try in the 1956 Challenge Cup final and former Welsh Rugby Union star Steve Llewellyn. Arguably the best uncapped winger in the game, with 240 tries in 287 appearances for St.Helens since signing in 1948, Llewellyn was nearing the end of his auspicious career. In the St.Helens Reporter, Tom Ashcroft suggested that only a major overhaul of the club's back division would see a return to more open football: *"The team is getting results in resolute style and is firmly planted in the top four, but it is a long time since the Saints were able to do any window dressing in the back line. Just as in showbusiness, a rugby league club does need a star attraction at reasonably regular intervals."*

Were you there?

Dateline Saturday 25th October 1957

Tom Van Vollenhoven scores his first try for St.Helens on his debut against Leeds at Knowsley Road. Other St.Helens players in the picture are (Left to right) Ray Price, Duggie Greenall and Walter Delves.

Rugby League was the abiding passion for thousands of 'Sintelliners' who followed the team home and away on a regular basis. Meanwhile, what better than a piping hot meal after the match courtesy of the latest GEC quality cooker with full-view glass door, storage drawer and auto timer-a snip at £10 15 Shillings (£10-75p). 'Invisible ray' speed traps had been introduced by the Police, cutting down the accident rate on local roads considerably!
Travelling by train was certainly cheap by today's standards, with a day-return ticket to Southport costing just 4 Shillings (20p). In the St.Helens Reporter, readers' questions on Russia's 'Sputnick 1' space probe were answered by a local boffin. American teen idol Paul Anka topped the charts with 'Diana', while cinemagoers at the Hippodrome were rocking in the aisles to the delights of Bill Hayley and the Comets in 'Don't Knock The Rock.' Dancing the night away with Bert Webb and his Band at the Coop Ballroom was also something to savour! For those who preferred to stay at home in the evenings, there was always the television. A 21 inch 'Console' with doors could be purchased for the sum of 104 Guineas from Radio Rentals in Westfield Street. Typical fayre? B.B.C. programmes included 'Watch With Mother' and 'Mainly For Women' in the afternoon. Light entertainment was provided by the 'Billy Cotton Bandshow' and 'Those Beverley Sisters.' On I.T.V. quiz shows like 'Take Your Pick' and 'Double Your Money' were popular. 'Emergency Ward Ten' was the compulsive soap opera of it's day!

SULLY THE POOLS WINNER!

Jim Sullivan was in no doubt that Vollenhoven was the man to revive flagging spectator interest at Knowsley Road. According to utility back Austin Rhodes, the Flying Springbok soon impressed his new team-mates: *"I remember his first training session when Jim Sullivan introduced him to us. We started doing some sprints and he was like lightening! We had a game of 'tick' rugby and he scooted in for four tries in quick succession. I said to Sully, 'Good God, you've got a jewel here!' He couldn't stop laughing-just like he had won the pools!"*

Despite Sullivan's optimism, Tom had not played for over two months and wondered whether he knew enough about rugby league to make his bow before the public after just a week in England. Yet Vollenhoven was given a rapturous welcome by over 23,000 Saints' fans when he made his intended debut against a powerful Leeds side at Knowsley Road on 26th.October 1957-on the right wing. His centre that day was the experienced Duggie Greenall, the former Great Britain international, who was under strict instructions to 'nurse' the Springbok through his first 80 minutes of professional rugby. Unfortunately, Tom's lack of knowledge of the game soon became apparent when he failed to cover a loose ball over his own try line. The ball was eagerly snapped up by centre Pat Quinn for a simple Leeds score. A hush of disappointment fell over the ground for several minutes. It proved to be the only blemish in an otherwise faultless St.Helens performance. There was no hint of the 'creeping barrage' as the re-vamped threequarter line scored all but one of the Saints' 8 tries in a storming 36-7 victory. Although scrum half Alex Murphy ran in a devastating hat-trick of tries, the principal architect of victory was veteran Welsh stand off Ray Price, signed from Warrington for a bargain £1,500 several weeks before. Indeed, he capped a fine performance with a try himself with five minutes to go. The major thrill was still to come, however, and the man that Leeds could not contain was the Originator-in-Chief once more. Still going for the gaps like a bullet, Price broke through on halfway with a minute to go. As he veered towards the right flank, the huge crowd sensed that this was the moment they had been waiting for. The roar of expectation increased in intensity as Price swept the ball to Vollenhoven nearly 40 yards from the line. The Van showed for the first time the catapult-like acceleration that was to become his trademark. Outpacing Broughton and Dunn with consummate ease, he crossed the line at the Scoreboard corner and touched down under the posts. The final whistle sounded shortly after Rhodes' conversion as the jubilant Saints' fans hailed the birth of a new Rugby League superstar. Vol. had well and truly arrived!

"The crowd were with him all the way," wrote Tom Ashcroft. *"They gasped at his bursts of speed, sighed where he was lacking in Rugby League knowhow, applauded his gameness and finally hailed the try with a roar as full-throated as the one that signalled Frank Carlton's winning try at Wembley in 1956."*

FIRST IMPRESSIONS

Naturally, Tom was delighted to mark his Saints' debut with a try-the end of a remarkable first week in a strange country and a new code of rugby. Ray Price, who was staying at the same guest house as Tom and Leonie, did much to help calm Tom's nerves before the kick off against Leeds. *"Yet the best tonic of all was that fine reception the crowd gave me as the Saints' team came out onto the field,"* he recalls. *"I did not know the supporters and they did not know me, or whether I was any good as a footballer. But they applauded me heartily and I felt at once as though I was among friends. I must confess that I was rather confused early on when Leeds scored. I should have picked the ball up or fallen on it. Ironically it was Pat Quinn, a member of the 1955 Lions in South Africa who scored for Leeds! The role of the winger in League did not seem to be all that much different from what I was used to in the 15-a-side game!"*

SAFE AT HOME

On account of his inexperience, Vol. was spared the rather daunting trip to Whitehaven's Recreation Ground seven days later and appeared in the Reserves, or 'A' Team against the Cumbrian club's Second String. The attraction of the Saints' new boy drew an incredible 8,500 fans to Knowsley Road. Tom joined what is arguably the fastest threequarter line ever assembled on any rugby league ground. His centre was Ken Large, ex-St.Helens Rugby Union Club, with a personal best of 10.1 for the 100 yards. In the other centre position was Sam Clempson (9.9), who just missed out on selection for the British Olympic Sprint team in 1956. Outside him was Derek Johnson, another 10.1 flyer, who later played on the wing for Hull at Wembley in 1960.

Although Vollenhoven did not receive a single pass in a drab first half, an aspiring young journalist called Keith Macklin reported how the blond-haired sensation set the ground alight in the 55th.minute: *"Large broke through brilliantly and whipped the ball out to Van Vollenhoven. He shot into his stride as if catapulted from an ejector seat and left three men clutching air and trailing in his wake as he flashed round under the posts for the try of the afternoon."* The Springbok Ace treated the large crowd to a further try from an interception in the last minute to seal a 33-23 victory for the Saints' Reserves.

LLEW'S INDIAN SUMMER!

Tom was back in the First Team against Swinton at Knowsley Road a week later. Former Saints' winger Steve Llewellyn recalls an amusing incident with Vollenhoven before the kick off: *"I was actually picked on the left wing for the first time in my career that day. We were going to play towards the Pavilion, so as left wing I ran across to the Main Stand. Vol. ran with me and stood next to me. Thinking back, Vol. had recognized that Llewellyn had played right wing for ten seasons or so-and that's where he's going to be-after all, he had played at Whitehaven the previous week. I remember turning him round to see which number he had on. It was number 2, so I said 'You're on the right wing, Tom.' I say to people, rather tongue-in-cheek, that Vol. might well have been as great a left winger as he was on the right. After all, he had been playing on the left wing in South Africa....and I might have had another season or two in rugby league!"*

Steve Llewellyn watched with admiration from the other flank as Tom scored a fantastic hat-trick in the 43-11 demolition of Swinton and really got the home fans behind him! On December 21st., Vol. equalled the club's individual try-scoring record with six at Knowsley Road against a shell-shocked Wakefield Trinity-and the tries just kept on coming! The Van roared in for 38 touchdowns in 30 appearances, a remarkable achievement in his first season as a professional. Even in those early days he could do no wrong. The possessor of an irresistible body swerve, most opponents were left for dead as he shot away towards the line! He had tremendous strength for his size to hand off and shrug himself clear of would-be tacklers.

Jim Sullivan predicted great things for the young South African and was positively in awe of his footballing talents. Steve Llewellyn watched Vollenhoven in one of his early matches in Yorkshire: *"I remember sitting on the bench at Hull when Vol. had one of his first runs down the touchline. As defenders came across to bury him, he warded them off with his hip. Sully said 'Did you see that - incredible!' He could ride tackles superbly and had phenomenal all-round ability."*

Here was a new manace to defences already being tested by the likes of Wigan's Billy Boston and the Warrington try-scoring machine Brian Bevan. *"He is a nugget, this boy Vollenhoven,"* wrote Tom Ashcroft. *"The sort who will go on bringing in the crowds and sending them home full of joyful reminiscence."* Prophetic words indeed!

STAR WARS

The Wigan Directors, stung by their failure to land Vollenhoven, responded immediately with the capture of Huddersfield and Great Britain winger Mick Sullivan for a world record £9,500 fee. Saints' swoop had seemingly left Wigan in a desperate mood and ready to pay £1,000 over the odds to get their man this time.

Despite the tremendous success of the South African venture, with gates averaging around 16,000 at Knowsley Road, the Saints were unable to lift a major trophy during the 1957/58 season. The team finished second in the league behind Oldham and were beaten by Workington at home in the Championship Semi-Final. Indeed, one of the shocks of the season saw unfancied Featherstone Rovers knock St.Helens out of the Challenge Cup by 5-0 in Arctic conditions at Post Office Road. Doubtless Vol. and the St.Helens' Directors were to cast rather envious glances in the direction of Central Park in the ensuing months, as Wigan went on to win the competition by beating Workington 13-9, with Mick Sullivan scoring a try! Wigan's Skipper and centre Eric Ashton, originally rejected by his home-town team became the first St.Helens-born player to receive the Challenge Cup at Wembley!

Burning the ground!
Tom scores one of his two tries in Saints' 29-6 victory against Workington at Knowsley Road on November 23rd 1957.
(St.Helens Reporter)

CHAPTER FIVE

TOP OF THE POPS

The remarkable success of Tom Van Vollenhoven's first season with the Saints was undoubtedly helped by the skill and expertise of his centre, Duggie Greenall. Although approaching the veteran stage, Duggie was the perfect partner for Vol., a great timer of a pass and the possessor of a mighty crash tackle which made him feared throughout the League - despite being barely eleven and a half stones wet through! *"Duggie was a great influence when I first arrived at Saints,"* remembers Tom. *"He said to me 'Stay on your wing and you will score tries.' He was right too! He was the perfect centre!"*

Off the field, Tom and Leonie had moved into their new home in Sackville Road, in the Windle District of St.Helens, about a mile from the rugby ground. In those early days, Tom was employed by Rothery Radio-a record shop in St.Helens Town Centre. Former Manager, the Late Les Charnock, remembered that having Tom on the payroll was good for business: *"People used to come into the shop to buy their favourite records and have a chat with the Saints' latest star. We used to have quite a few big names from the music business who came into the shop doing promotional work. I remember Tom driving the American singing star Emile Ford to one particular charity 'do'. They were good times. Tom and I used to go to the Y.M.C.A. for lunch every day and have a game of table tennis. We would also go tenpin bowling at Burtonwood Airbase. When Tom eventually left Rothery's, our record sales plummeted for a good while afterwards!"*

THE GREAT ARTISTE

Peter Harvey, a former team-mate of Vollenhoven's at St.Helens in the 'Sixties, gives a revealing insight into the South African's early career at Knowsley Road: *"When Tom signed for Saints, I was a 17 year-old training with Liverpool Rugby Union Club. Our Captain was Reg Higgins, who had been on the 1955 Tour to South Africa. I asked him what Vollenhoven was like. Reg replied 'The people of St.Helens do not know just how good this fellow is-probably the best player in the world!' That was his quote even before Tom arrived in this country! After such a recommendation, I was looking forward to seeing a classy player. I watched him from the terraces when I was 17/18-that was probably the best time, the first three years. He was literally magic. I used to go behind the goals to watch him, rather than the Popular Side. It was best to watch the great man running in a straight line to appreciate his magic-because Vol. could run in a straight line and beat people with his change of pace. He would take a line five yards off the touchline which gave him enough room on the outside if he wanted it. Then he would hold his line and actually stop people as they ran at him-and then accelerate away. I could never quite work out how he did it! Even when we played together for the Saints I would be asking myself 'How did he do that?' It was just artistry and with Vol. you were looking at an artist. Like all true art you can't analyse it. You do not know why true art is good, you just look at it and say that something is much better than the other. In Tom's case it was the ease with which he did everything and the ability to change pace when*

"You've never had it so good!"

everyone else was running flat out. He used to do it to us in training-he would just accelerate away, like Seb Coe used to do in his pomp. You could see him change gear because his head would go to one side. That was Vol. stepping up from threequarter pace to overdrive! When you thought he was running flat out-and as people went in to tackle him-he would accelerate away. Defensively, too, he was brilliant. If he could take out the opposing centre, he would do so. If he had a 'two-on-one' against him, however, he would back off initially and appear to give the centre a chance by turning momentarily towards the winger. As the centre took another couple of strides, Vol. would run back and take him out-a wonderful defensive technique!"

A RED LETTER DAY!

'You've never had it so good,' the catchphrase made famous by Prime Minister Harold Mc.Millan in the late 1950s, had particular relevance for St.Helens supporters during the 1958/59 season-both on and off the field! Saturday, August 23rd., 1958 provided further evidence of the club's newly-found status among the Rugby League elite when a magnificent new £32,000 grandstand was opened before the first match of the season against Featherstone Rovers. The Saints duly christened their new showpiece with an emphatic 32-9 victory against the Yorkshiremen. Inevitably it was

Vollenhoven who brought patrons to their feet time and time again with some breathtaking runs. The first of his two tries, which began with a Greenall pass in his own half, showed the mark of a true genius. Vol. accelerated down the touchline leaving Kinsey floundering like a sinking swimmer, and with less than a yard to work in, he side-stepped outside Elford, veered in and crossed the line 20 yards from the posts on the new grandstand side. Tom was not content just to ground the ball! He swerved effortlessly past another opponent inside the try area to ground the ball with geometric precision under the posts. Crowd pleasers like Tom Van Vollenhoven would ensure the financial success of the new stand for many years to come!

COME AND JOIN US!

Tom Van Vollenhoven's success at St.Helens was a vital factor in the recruitment of star players to the club, especially those from Rugby Union. As Peter Harvey remembers: *"The Saints first tried to sign me in 1959, after I had captained England Schoolboys' Rugby Union side. I decided to go to college first-there was always the chance of honours at senior international level. I went to see Chairman Harry Cook in the Boardroom and he says 'Just imagine...if you sign for us you could be centre to Vollenhoven.' That was quite an incentive for any player to turn professional!"*

In October, 1958, increased gate receipts meant that the Saints could pay out a record fee for a forward of £7,250 to secure rampaging second-rower Dick Huddart from Whitehaven. In the same month, the St.Helens Board announced another venture into South African Rugby Union with the £4,000 signing of Springbok left winger Johannes Albertus (Jan) Prinsloo. The Saints had first approached him in January, 1958, before he had become an international. According to Jan's Agent, former Halifax forward Jack Pansegrouw, the time was now right for him to turn professional. A Detective Sergeant in the South African Police, the 23 year old had a best time of 9.6 for the 100 yards, set in the Police Championships-and once competed against Vollenhoven, returning 9.9 seconds to Tom's 9.8! In a letter to Pansegrouw, Saints' Secretary Basil Lowe was quick to point out the success of the club's previous venture: *"I think I can tell you that Tom Van Vollenhoven is very happy here with us. He regrets in no way signing for this club and loves his football. He has recently had an addition to the family (a girl) and his wife is very happy in this country."*

At 5ft. 11ins. and over 13 stones the sturdily-built flyer was virtually unstoppable with the line in his sights. There was press speculation that Tom would be switched back to his original position of centre to accomodate him. Although Coach Jim Sullivan considered such a pairing at one stage, Prinsloo took over the left wing spot and was an instant success, scoring twice on his debut against Rochdale Hornets on November 8th.

RUGBY RECORD BREAKERS

Buoyed by their two ex-Springboks, the Saints produced some of their best-ever attacking football in 1958/59, shattering several long-standing records in the process. St.Helens headed the league table with a five point margin over rivals Wigan and in 35 matches scored 1,005 points-215 tries and 180 goals, the highest-ever league total at the time. There were mixed fortunes in the cup competitions, however. In the Lancashire Cup Final at Swinton-Tom Van Vollenhoven's first major final appearance for St.Helens-the 'Roughyeds' of Oldham rendered the Saints' attacking machine try-less in a 12-2 defeat in front of 38,780 fans. The biggest blow came in the third round of the Challenge Cup at Featherstone, where, for the second successive year, Saints' hopes nosedived, to the tune of 20-6 ! Although Prinsloo finished the campaign with an impressive tally of 27 tries from 29 appearances, it was Tom Van Vollenhoven who stole the spotlight with his incredible scoring feats. In his first full season, the Flying Springbok topped the league's try-scoring charts with 62 touchdowns and broke the club record of 55 formerly held by Great Britain International winger Alf

Great Expectations!
Tom and Skipper Duggie Greenall (centre with ball) put Jan Prinsloo through his paces on the famous Knowsley Road Turf.

Ellaby. 'Vanishing' Vol's second try in the league match against Workington on April 22nd., 1959 smashed the 32 year old record as the Saints cruised to a 36-14 victory.

AGAINST ALL ODDS!

Unlike today, there was no recognition for finishing in first place in the league table. The top four sides played off against each other to reach the Championship Final-the supreme accolade at the end of a long, hard season. St.Helens destroyed fourth-placed Oldham by 42-4 at Knowsley Road, despite the noteable absence of Vollenhoven with a hamstring injury and went into a testing final against Hunslet at Odsal Stadium, Bradford. This was not only the club's last chance for honours, but Coach Jim Sullivan's final match in charge-two reasons why success was most desireable! Such was Tom's importance to the rest of the team, however, that he played with his troublesome left thigh heavily bandaged-hard to believe that the South African Superstar was about to take centre stage in the greatest Championship Final of them all!

The Hunslet contingent in the huge 50,000 crowd had plenty to cheer about in the opening quarter, when Stockdill and Doyle touched down for tries and full back Langton kicked three goals, as the Yorkshiremen surged into a 12-4 lead. 'Club Standard' Hunslet, as one critic dubbed them, were poised to finish off the star-spangled Saints, when out of nothing Vollenhoven conjured up an astonishing solo effort which totally altered the course of the game. The Flying Springbok had 75 yards to travel and a couple of feet along the touchline in which to work, with the Hunslet cover defenders closing in rapidly. A breathtaking change of pace left

Team of all talents

St.Helens R.L.F.C. 1958-59

The St.Helens team line up for the photographer before the 42-14 demolition of Rochdale Hornets at Knowsley Road on November 8th. 1958. Vollenhoven (3), Prinsloo (2), Murphy (2), Howard (2) and Greenall were the Saints' try-scorers. Fearis kicked 6 goals. Back Row L to R: DICK HUDDART, a rampaging second rower, who cost a record £7,250 from Whitehaven.12 appearances for Great Britain and an Australian tourist in 1958 and 1962. TOM GRUNDY, prop forward. Local lad from a famous rugby family. JAN PRINSLOO, a former South African Rugby Union international winger making a double try-scoring debut for the St.Helens club. Later joined Wakefield and died tragically of a heart attack in 1966. TOM VAN VOLLENHOVEN, the most exciting winger in the game, who went on to establish a new club record of 62 tries in a season. ALBERT TERRY, at over 16 stones, remarkably agile for a prop forward. Great Britain tourist in 1958. Later joined Leeds and Castleford. BRIAN BRIGGS, second row ace signed from Huddersfield. Transferred to Wakefield in 1960. PETER FEARIS, goalkicking centre signed from Blackpool Borough. Equalled club record with 13 goals in Saints' 71-15 thrashing of Barrow on 14th.February 1959. WALTER DELVES, stand-in hooker for Great Britain international Tom Mc.Kinney in this match. Normally a second rower or loose forward.

Front Row L to R: VINCE KARALIUS, a granite-like loose forward, dubbed the 'Wild Bull of the Pampas' by the Australians. Widnes born of Lithuanian extraction. GLYN MOSES, the 'Prince of Full Backs,' Great Britain tourist in 1958. An inspirational signing by Coach Jim Sullivan in 1952 after a spell out of the game. ALEX MURPHY, the greatest scrum half of his generation. Supremely confident. Thatto Heath born, toured Australia in 1958 while still a teenager; DUGGIE GREENALL, centre and Captain. One of the hardest men ever to play Rugby League. Great Britain tourist and the perfect partner for Tom Van Vollenhoven during his early career at Knowsley Road. BRIAN HOWARD, stand off. A stocky, hard-running utility back who later joined Leigh. Son Harvey Howard starred for Widnes in the 1990s.

We are the Champions! Jubilant dressing room scenes at Odsal after the 44-22 defeat of Hunslet. Left to right: Duggie Greenall (Capt.), Brian Briggs, Austin Rhodes, Tom Van Vollenhoven, Dick Huddart and Alex Murphy.

three would-be tacklers clutching thin air. A change of direction sent another flying into the crowd at ringside. A jackhammer hand-off sent a fifth crashing to the turf and Vanishing Vol. crossed the line where he beat yet another Hunslet player, to touch down as near as possible to the posts.

It was one of the most spectacular tries in Rugby League history and archetypal Vollenhoven, who always seemed capable of producing something extra-ordinary when the chips were down. A conversion by full-back Rhodes and a penalty goal shortly afterwards put further pressure on a now fast-wilting Hunslet side. Vol.'s 25th. minute masterpiece had turned the game around completely, as the Saints really got into their normal groove of devastating attacking football. *"That was one hell of a long try to score in the circumstances,"* recalls Tom. *"I was really struggling with the hamstring. I went back to South Africa for a holiday shortly afterwards and the leg was black and blue. I could hardly walk for the next few weeks or so. We were really playing badly at the time and the crowd were growing more and more anxious. It seemed to inspire the whole team. After that we really went to town....!"*
In the 33rd.minute, scrum half Alex Murphy nudged St.Helens ahead with a typical opportunist try which Rhodes converted once more. There was no stopping the Saints with their noses in front at 16-12 and Jan Prinsloo finished off a sparkling six-man move by crashing in at the corner for try number three. Just before half time, Vollenhoven picked up his second try to give St.Helens a commanding 24-12 lead at half time. Despite some obvious discomfort from his injury, it took a mere two minutes of the second half for Vollenhoven to complete a glorious hat-trick. There was even more to enjoy for the thousands of St.Helens' fans basking in the early Summer sun as Sully's Glory Boys went on to break all records with 8 tries and 10 goals in their sensational 44-22 victory!

CHAMPIONSHIP FINAL
ST.HELENS 44 HUNSLET 22
ODSAL STADIUM, BRADFORD
SATURDAY 16TH.MAY, 1959
ST.HELENS Rhodes (10 goals); Van Vollenhoven (3 tries), Greenall, Mc.Ginn, Prinsloo (try); Smith (try), Murphy (2 tries); Terry, Mc.Kinney, Prescott (Capt.), Briggs, Huddart (try), Karalius.
HUNSLET Langton (5 goals); Colin, Stockdill (try), Preece, Walker; Gabbitas, Doyle (try); Hatfield, Smith, Eyre, Poole (try), Gunney (try), Shaw.
Referee: Wilson (Dewsbury)
Attendance: 50,562

As part of a series entitled 'The Best of the 20th.Century' in the Guardian Newspaper, on February 11th.1993, 'Centipede' chose Vollenhoven's magnificent solo effort at Odsal as the 'Try of the Century' in both codes of rugby...describing it as *"The non pareil of verve, nerve, balance and strength."* Praise indeed!

HAIL THE CONQUERING HERO

At the final whistle ecstatic St.Helens supporters singled out Vollenhoven as their hero and carried him shoulder high in triumph from the field. Yet there were other great individual performances that afternoon, not least from scrum half Alex Murphy, prop forward Ab Terry and Saints' formidable back row trio of Briggs, Huddart and Karalius.

Hail the conquering hero! Saints' Chairman Harry Cook presents Tom Van Vollenhoven to an ecstatic crowd outside the Town Hall on the team's return from the 1959 Championship Final at Odsal.

Over 5,000 fans gathered in Victoria Square that evening to welcome back their team-and one man in particular-with chants of 'We want the Van!' The Mayor made several attempts to begin his speech, but the crowd would not have it until Vollenhoven, the hero of the day, had been forced to step forward to acknowledge the rapturous applause. After the team had taken a bow, including veteran centre Duggie Greenall-who had been rejuvenated since the signing of Vollenhoven-the last words rested, appropriately, with a delighted Jim Sullivan: *"Nobody will begrudge us our victory. We have been there all season and I am thrilled we have done it!"* Great days indeed. Saints' supporters truly 'Never had it so good!"

CHAPTER SIX

Simply the best!

RUNNING ON EMPTY

"What has Tom Van Vollenhoven, the Saints' creator of headlines, lost in pace and staying power during his off-season stay in his native country? That was the question which transcended all others after Saints had whipped Blackpool Borough 59-17 on Monday night," Wrote Tom Ashcroft in the St.Helens Reporter on 17th.August, 1959. *"The crowd stood aghast as they watched a relative unknown wing opponent, Alan Meadows, twice overhaul the ex-Springbok after he had broken clear. The infallible idol, previously regarded as unchallengable in the matter of speed, was human after all. On most occasions he has been able to discount the disadvantage of carrying the ball, but when he failed to score, Vollenhoven was five yards in a hundred slower than at his best and his ability to cover unlimited distances was reduced."*

Such was Tom's reputation in the game, that being caught by a winger from such a lowly club as Blackpool Borough caused a sensation! His opponent, Alan Meadows, was St.Helens-born and a former member of the famous Sutton Harriers Athletic Club. As Tom explains, he was not at his best: *"I trained with Mike Holt, a welterweight boxing champion back home in South Africa that Summer. He lived near my parents and every morning we would jog around the rugby field. Unfortunately, apart from keeping me reasonably fit, this type of running took the edge off my pace. I was quite sluggish when I returned to England and it took me a few weeks to build up my speed again."*
In other respects against Blackpool, however, Tom was at his superb best. He scored four tries, beating opponents all the way to the line on each occasion with his customary ease. *"Yet the fickle views of a rugby crowd,"* added Ashcroft, *"are such that these accomplishments were considered subsidiary to the one decline in his powers."* Clearly, the form of Rugby League's latest superstar now warranted the most intensive scrutiny from the media and supporters alike!

Despite such an early season hiccup, the Flying Springbok was soon back to his bewildering best. The speed-particularly the ability to find that extra gear-returned and he finished the 1959/60 campaign with 54 tries from 42 matches, the League's leading scorer for the second successive season!

IN A LEAGUE OF THEIR OWN

As the fifties drew to a close, Rugby League fans had the probably never-to-be-repeated opportunity of watching three of the greatest practitioners of wing play that the Game has ever seen. Tom Van Vollenhoven, a superstar less than two years after turning professional, Wigan's 'Blockbuster' Billy Boston and the Warrington Marvel, Brian Bevan-all right wingers-vied for top spot in the scoring charts. It was a measure of the opportunities provided by an attack-minded St.Helens side, coupled with Tom's exceptional finishing ability, that he was able to retain his position as the league's leading try-scorer at the end of the 1959/60 season with 54 tries. Boston was his nearest challenger with 47, while Bevan, arguably past his best, notched 40 touchdowns in third place. Yet both Tom's rivals were to have a strong say in the destination of two major

Simply the best!
Tom with the Evening Chronicle Player of the Year Trophy.

trophies that the Saints were favourites to lift during the campaign.

A former stoker in the Australian Navy, Brian Bevan was signed by Warrington just after the War and in 18 seasons with the Wires, Blackpool Borough and the Other Nationalities XIII amassed a world record of 796 tries! Bev. totally belied the appearance of being a top class athlete. Yet this thin, balding figure, seemingly held together by knee and elbow bandages possessed dazzling acceleration, a brilliant side-step and an insatiable appetite for tries. *"Bev. was a remarkable try-scorer who possessed a fine pair of hands,"* remembers former Saints' winger Steve Llewellyn. *"Yet most of all he knew how to sidestep without losing much pace. The number of tries he scored at the corner without being tackled, sometimes squeezing in, putting the ball down, other times anchors down and with the full back past him he would simply walk over and put the ball down. On a one-to-one he was absolutely deadly. I remember Glyn Moses - a great defensive full back - throwing up his hands in total exasperation before Bev went past him during one match at Knowsley Road!"*

Despite the ability to score tries from virtually anywhere on the field, Bevan-unlike Vollenhoven-was not renowned for his defensive qualities. *"There is no doubt whatsoever who was the greatest try-scorer,"* recalls Stan Mc.Cormick, a former team-mate of Bevan, who went on to coach Vollenhoven at St.Helens. *"Although Bevan was quite a hard man in his own right, Tom was more robust. He was certainly the greater all-round winger. It's like saying Gary Lineker is the greatest goalscorer.....but there are better centre forwards!"*
Bev and the Van were to clash in the 1959 Lancashire Cup Final between Warrington and St.Helens at Central Park, Wigan, where the Wires snatched an unexpected-and controversial-victory! In the 30th.minute of a tough-tackling encounter, Warrington left winger Terry O'Grady fielded the ball on his own '25' and crashed through two attempted tackles. After a near-60 yard run, he fed the supporting Greenough, who put in a short kick towards the right-hand corner. In a moment of high drama for the 39,237 spectators, Greenough's path had been partially blocked by Rhodes, as Vollenhoven, Prinsloo and Bevan led the chase, the latter intent upon scoring the 698th try of his career! The Saints' wingers reached the ball first in an upright position. Bev slid in between them on the wet turf, for referee Coates to signal what was to become the winning touchdown in Warrington's 5-4 success. A photograph of the incident shows Vollenhoven in front of Bevan with left arm raised as he prepared to boot the ball away. Even a recently-unearthed film of the incident, taken from behind the dead-ball line is inconclusive. The decision certainly could have gone either way! After the match, Tom insisted that Bevan did not get a hand to the ball, although in view of the Saints' overall performance that day, it was hardly necessary to elevate the dispute to the level of a cause celebre! As it turned out, there were bigger disappointments to come!

YOU GET NOWT FOR BEING...FIRST!

Although Brian Bevan was nearing the end of his illustrious career, Billy Boston was, like Vollenhoven, enjoying phenomenal success. Both Saints and Wigan had powerful sides and were always in contention for major honours. Given the tremendous rivalry between the two clubs, it was only natural that their man was the best right winger in the Game! Born in Cardiff's Tiger Bay, Billy Boston joined Wigan in 1953 from Forces Rugby Union for £3,000 - a staggering fee for a non-international player....and made such an impression that he toured Australia with Great Britain at the end of his first full season! By the dawn of the Sixties, Boston's once lithe, sinewy form had filled out to over 15 stones. This, coupled with his great pace made him extremely difficult to stop at full throttle. He had a surprisingly deft side-step, outside swerve and possessed a jackhammer hand-off. Yet Billy also developed a fearsome crash tackle that would take out the opposing centre with precision timing. He could turn out at stand off and centre with equal aplomb and his build meant that he could play in the forwards if required!

At the end of the 1959/60 League campaign, the Saints had finished as leaders once more, 13 points clear of Wigan, in fourth place. On May 7th., the two rivals clashed at Knowsley Road in the Championship Semi-Final. After 20 minutes, with the scores tied at 2-2, a fantastic handling movement by the Saints' threequarter line saw centre Ken Large put Vollenhoven in for a converted try. Then came the incident which shattered Saints' composure and their grip on the match. Alex Murphy became involved in a fracas with Wigan's Mick Sullivan, normally a winger, who had been moved to stand off to do a special marking job on the St.Helens danger man. Both players were promptly sent off by referee Eric 'Sergeant Major' Clay! Wigan responded immediately with a Boston try just before half-time and a Griffiths penalty after 49 minutes levelled the scores at 7-7. On the hour another Griffiths goal inched them into the lead. It was then that Boston stole the show by crashing through several attempted tackles to score a crucial three-pointer, despite the efforts of Vollenhoven, who had rushed over from the other flank to try and cover the danger! Wigan went on to win by 19-9 and lifted the Championship Trophy in the Final against Wakefield shortly afterwards. By way of consolation, the Saints had won the Lancashire League title at a canter, 9 points ahead of the Riversiders-yet in cup-tie football had failed to deliver the goods. Tom's hopes of Challenge Cup success had also evaporated, with a first round defeat at the hands of Wakefield Trinity! Yet Wembley glory-and revenge over deadly rivals Wigan-was just over the horizon.

OLD RIVALS...GOOD FRIENDS

Some thirty years later, in October 1990, Tom returned to St.Helens to take part in the Saints' Ground Centenary Celebrations and met up with his old adversary Billy Boston at Central Park. Memories came flooding back for both men as they looked towards the famous pitch. *"Tom's going to pull me up about the time I knocked his teeth out,"* recalled Billy. *"It only seems like yesterday. We were playing Saints at Knowsley Road and I saw Tom flying down the wing in typical fashion. He was a natural try-scorer, but there was no way through on this occasion! I must have caught him with a really good belt, but it was a case of giving as much as you got in those days!"*
Tom replied:
"I wondered what had hit me and then remember Billy coming into our dressing room at the end of the game and being ever so apologetic. I had to laugh at his manner, but it's like Billy says-you gave as good as you got. Strength was Billy's forte. He was immensely powerful and it took up to six to knock him down. I guess that it was good for the fans with Billy at Wigan and me doing my bit for the Saints. We were rivals on the field but always the best of friends off it!"

VOL THE SUPREME ATHLETE

Given that Bevan is the greatest try-scorer, it is rather more difficult to ascertain whether Vollenhoven or Boston should assume the mantle of the Game's most complete wing threequarter. One indisputable fact is that for three seasons, 1958/59, 1959/60 and 1960/61-Tom Van Vollenhoven was the League's number one winger. Until the advent of Martin Offiah in the late 1980s., no other winger had achieved three successive seasons, post-war, at the top of the try-scoring charts-especially with such top quality opposition around. In sheer aesthetic terms, however, there was no finer sight than to see Tom running at speed-perfectly balanced and using his deceptive strength to fend off potential tacklers. *"I was extremely flattered when the Late Ron Pickering used me as a role model in a film on balanced running,"* recalls Tom. *"He filmed me first of all on the track and then playing rugby....he called me the perfectly balanced athlete!"*

Peter Harvey remembers one amazing incident before a training session just after he had joined the Saints in 1963: *"I was with Tom, Alex Murphy, Len Killeen and Keith Northey. I mentioned that before matches at Loughborough College, we P.E. students used to warm up by doing spring flick-flacks and backward somersaults to try and put the opposition off-just for a laugh. Then Tom says 'Do you mean like this?' He did it perfectly! Vol. was a gymnast. He had great balance, power and overall athleticism. Everyone knows he ran 10.6 for the 100 yards, but he was also a 54 feet hop, step and jumper, which means he had tremendous leg power. Put all those things together and you have a formidable all-round athlete-the sort of background to explain why he could do what he did. He was in total control of his body balance. He was strong in the thigh-and in the upper body also. I remember one match when Wigan full-back Ray Ashby got hold of Tom in a bear-hug tackle. Volly just pushed him away from the inside of the tackle. He could get out of tackles with sheer strength!"*

PUTTING ON THE STYLE

As the 1960/61 season got under way, the old order was changing at Knowsley Road. The man who had done so much to propel the Saints into the 'Big league,' Jim Sullivan, had rather surprisingly taken up the coaching reins at Rochdale Hornets twelve months before. He was replaced by the legendary prop forward Alan Prescott, whose playing career had just come to an end. Tom's early mentor in the centre, Duggie Greenall, had joined Wigan and a new partnership was emerging with another local lad, Ken Large. A star sprinter, signed from local Rugby Union, Large's pace and vision helped to establish one of the most lethal attacking combinations in the League.
This devastating partnership was prominent as St.Helens reached their third successive Lancashire Cup Final, against Swinton at Central Park on October 29th. 1960. Large was instrumental in sending his partner away for the first try in the 11th.minute of a thrilling encounter. Large also got his name on the scoresheet as the Saints-with scrum half Alex Murphy celebrating his first weekend pass from the R.A.F. in storming form-triumphed by 15-9.

LANCASHIRE CUP FINAL
ST.HELENS 15 SWINTON 9
AT CENTRAL PARK, WIGAN
SATURDAY 29TH.OCTOBER 1960
ST.HELENS Landsberg; Van Vollenhoven (try), Large (try), Mc.Ginn, Prinsloo; Rhodes (try, 3 goals), Murphy; Terry, Dagnall, Leyland, Vines, Huddart, Karalius (Capt.)

SWINTON Gowers; Speed, Smethurst, Buckley, Mc.Gregor (try); Parkinson, Dyson; Bretherton, T.Roberts, Moses, K.Roberts, Norburn, Blan (Capt. 3 goals).
Referee: Clay (Rothwell)
Attendance: 31,755

MARCHING ON TO WEMBLEY!

Tom needed just one more winner's medal to complete his collection-in the 'blue riband' of rugby league competitions-the Challenge Cup. Despite a Vollenhoven try, unfancied Widnes came away from Knowsley Road with a creditable 5-5 draw in a dour first round tie. In the replay, however, the Saints produced a champagne display of attacking rugby to swamp Widnes to the tune of 29-10! Vollenhoven, Large and Murphy each notched a brace of touchdowns, while recent £11,000 signing from Wigan, Mick Sullivan pitched in with try number seven. The march to the 'Twin Towers' had begun in style! Forty eight hours later, Tom Van Vollenhoven continued to be the 'Scourge of the Chemics' as he scorched in for 5 tries as the Saints thrashed Widnes 44-7 in a League match at Knowsley Road-the third time the sides had met in seven days!

The Great All Rounder!
No mean tackler, Vollenhoven halts the progress of Widnes full back Arthur Pimblett during Saints' 44-7 League victory at Knowsley Road, 18th February 1961. Tom also notched five tries during the match - finishing at it's best!
(St.Helens Reporter)

In Round Two, Castleford were beaten at Wheldon Road with another Vollenhoven brace, while a Dick Huddart 'special' turned the tide in an action-packed quarter final clash at home to Swinton. The St.Helens' squad rested at Ilkley before their semi-final clash with Hull at Bradford. An all-ticket crowd of 42,000 saw Vollenhoven smash the Humbersiders' bid for a second successive Wembley appearance with a stunning 50 yard solo touchdown which set the Saints on the way to a 26-9 success. The stage was now set for the 'Final of the Century'-St.Helens versus Wigan, the most compelling derby clash of them all!

BATTLE OF THE GIANTS

Both St.Helens and Wigan contained some of the biggest names in Rugby League football and the prospect of some intriguing individual battles created enormous interest in the neighbouring towns. Nowhere was this more apparent than on the flanks, characterised by the explosive clash between Saints' tough-tackling Mick Sullivan and ex team-mate Billy Boston, the most powerful threequarter in the game. On the other flank, Vollenhoven was faced by his former colleague Frank Carlton, who had joined Wigan earlier in the season for a bargain £5,000 fee.

Although cup-holders Wigan began as slight favourites, there seemed little to choose between the two sides. Wigan Captain Eric Ashton gave a somewhat prophetic summary of how the cup might be won in the pre-match Evening Chronicle Wembley Souvenir: *"Saints have a better chance of turning the game against the run of play. Wigan could be well on top but not scoring and Saints could come away suddenly with an individual Murphy or Vollenhoven effort and get themselves five points up."*

Temperatures had soared into the high 80s. by the time the teams entered the arena and most of the 95,000 crowd were in shirt-sleeve order, sweating profusely. During the predictably fierce opening exchanges, it was Wigan who gained first blood with a penalty from their South African full-back Fred 'Punchy' Griffiths. In the 32nd.minute, Eric Ashton's fears were realised as Huddart opened up a huge gap in the Wigan defence for Alex Murphy to romp over from just inside the '25.' Although full-back Rhodes was wide with the conversion, he kicked a towering penalty goal from half-way to give the Saints a vital 3 point lead with five minutes to go before half time.

POETRY IN MOTION

A further Griffiths penalty after 45 minutes reduced the arrears to a single point as Wigan threw everything into attack. The Saints, who drank a special cocktail of lemonade, salt and water at half time, survived only with the help of some desperate cover-tackling. Yet St.Helens always seemed capable of producing that little bit extra and with 17 minutes to go, laid claim to victory with one of the finest tries ever seen at Wembley Stadium. Dick Huddart pounced on a loose ball as a Wigan attack broke down ten yards from the Saints' line. Murphy moved the ball wide to Ken Large who beat two opponents with a sizzling burst of speed and passed to Vollenhoven on half-way. The Flying Springbok accelerated away from Carlton and, seeing his way blocked by Griffiths, gave a return pass inside to the supporting Large. The Saints' pair kept up a scorching pace along the touchline and as two red-shirted defenders raced across in a desperate attempt to cover, Large whipped the ball outside to Vollenhoven once more, who streaked away to touch down between the posts-a magnificent display of controlled running and passing at speed-pure Wembley magic!

Austin Rhodes kicked the goal and at 10-4 Wigan were a beaten side. The Saints' full back later crowned a memorable victory with a 40 yard penalty goal, after Murphy had been obstructed. Griffiths notched a consolation two-pointer with a penalty one minute from time, to make the final score 12-6.

CHALLENGE CUP FINAL
ST.HELENS 12 WIGAN 6
AT WEMBLEY STADIUM
SATURDAY 13TH.MAY 1961

ST.HELENS Rhodes (3 goals); Van Vollenhoven (try), Large, Mc.Ginn, Sullivan; Murphy (try), Smith; Terry, Dagnall, Watson, Vines, Huddart, Karalius (Capt.).

WIGAN Griffiths (3 goals); Boston, Ashton (Capt.), Bootle, Carlton; Bolton, Entwhistle; Barton, Sayer, Mc.Tigue, Lyon, Coilier, Evans.

Referee: Watkinson (Swinton)
Attendance: 94,672
Receipts: £38,479
Lance Todd Trophy: Huddart (Saints)

Every conceivable vantage point in Victoria Square was taken up on Monday evening as 20,000 ecstatic fans welcomed back their favourites before the Civic Reception at the Town Hall. There was a thunderous roar as Skipper Vince Karalius showed off the spoils of victory to the near-hysterical gathering, who demanded-and got-better views of

Wembley Magic!

Proud St.Helens skipper Vince Karalius holds the Challenge Cup aloft after the 12-6 defeat of deadly rivals Wigan.

Back row (L to R) Don Vines, Mick Sullivan, Alex Murphy, Cliff Watson, Dick Huddart, Bob Dagnall and Abe Terry.

Front row Tom Van Vollenhoven, Brian McGinn, Wilf Smith, Ken Large and Austin Rhodes.

their match-winning idols Huddart and Vollenhoven. After congratulations from the Mayor Councillor Joseph Murphy, the last words belonged to Saints' Chairman Harry Cook: *"Ours was a faster and fitter team and played the better football in defeating a great Wigan side. Lord Derby told me that he considered the Saints' two tries were perfect examples of intelligent and unselfish rugby. I think the game did a lot for Rugby League all over the country. "*

Yet the try fashioned with such skill by Tom and his centre partner remains one of the most memorable in the long history of Challenge Cup Finals at Wembley. *"Apparently Ken didn't expect me to pass the ball back to him,"* recalls Tom. *"Then, when he could see Eric Ashton on his heels he returned the compliment-it was great to score in such circumstances, especially against the 'Old Enemy' Wigan!"* This epic derby clash, including the 63rd.minute gem, was shown 'live' on B.B.C.s. Grandstand Saturday afternoon sports programme. How appropriate that a nationwide television audience should witness Tom Van Vollenhoven's ultimate achievement in Rugby League football. Indeed, Tom's 59th. try of the season secured his place at the top of the try-scoring charts for the third successive year. At that moment in time, the Flying Springbok was, quite simply, the best in the business!

TOP TWENTY TRYSCORERS-1960/61

59 T.Van Vollenhoven (St.Helens)
44 W.Rosenberg (Leeds)
37 W.Boston (Wigan)
35 B.Bevan (Warrington)
31 B Greenhough (Warrington)
31 A.Murphy (St.Helens)
31 J.Stopford (Swinton)
29 J.Freeman (Halifax)
26 J.Challinor (Warrington)
26 J.O'Neill (Workington)
25 A.Buckley (Swinton)
23 E.Ashton (Wigan)
23 F.Carlton (St.Helens/Wigan)
23 A.Hardisty (Castleford)
23 J.Noon (Oldham)
23 G.Paul (Hull K.R.)
23 I.Southward (Workington)
22 M.Martyn (Leigh)
21 D.Hallas (Leeds)
21 J.Prinsloo (St.Helens/Wakefield)

Wembley Here We Come!
Tom roars in for a magnificent solo try in the 29-6 demolition of Hull in the 1961 Challenge Cup Semi-Final at Bradford.

CHAPTER SEVEN

The South African gold rush!

THE SPRINGBOK CONNECTION

Such was Tom Van Vollenhoven's phenomenal success in the professional code that it was not long before the Saints' Directors continued their search for South African 'gold', with other top clubs following suit. What followed, in the late Fifties and early Sixties, was a small scale invasion of South African talent eager to try their hand at Rugby League. Their impact on the British game was rather erratic, however, principally a result of the difficulty in adjusting to the colder climate as well as to a new code of rugby! The casualty rate was high, with some big names biting the dust! Springbok scrum half Tommy Gentles, a team-mate of Vollenhoven's against the 1955 British Lions, was a spectacular big-money flop with Wigan-the club who had first explored the South African market, with some success, in the mid-1920s!

On Saturday, 1st.March 1958 the St.Helens Reporter announced the signing of a second South African player, on the heels of Vollenhoven: *"Like successful managers in show business, the Saints' Directors realise the value of introducing a new top line as often as they can. On Tuesday night, with a theatrical flourish, they described the capture of Ted Brophy, the North Transvaal forward who has also played for Transvaal. Brophy, a fitter from the Johannesburg district, moved north to work in the copper mines like Vollenhoven ...."*
A rough and ready character, best remembered for a daredevil-and near suicidal-leap from the Runcorn-Widnes railway bridge, Ted made just two first team appearances before moving on to Blackpool Borough and Leigh. Certainly the transition from Union to League can be more difficult for forwards and it was no surprise that the Saints opted for threequarter Jan Prinsloo as their next South African capture. Jan won many admirers at Knowsley Road before his transfer to Wakefield Trinity for £9,000 in January 1961-a record for the Yorkshire club at the time. Indeed, Wakefield made their own South African connections with the signing of threequarters Alan Skene, Colin Greenwood and Gert 'Oopa' Coetzer-who remains the last South African to play in a Challenge Cup Final, for Wakefield against Leeds in the infamous 'watersplash' Wembley encounter of 1968.

In January, 1959, the Saints' Directors called a special meeting to discuss the change of terms asked for the signing of Wilf Rosenberg. Tom's former centre and room-mate on the 1956 Springbok tour to Australia and New Zealand wanted "£3,500 tax-free signing payment, plus £500 university fees, small furnished flat, part rental to be paid." The St.Helens Board later

Danger - Genius at work!
Tom Van Vollenhoven torments the Blackpool Borough defence at Knowsley Road in the early 1960s. Stan Owen (left) and ex-Saints' South African prop Ted Brophy are about to bow to the inevitable!

agreed not to sign the player on the terms offered. Unlike Tom, Rosenberg's father came to England to negotiate a contract for him. Wilf signed for Leeds and used a large slice of his signing on fee to continue his studies in dentistry at Leeds Dental College. Such was Wilf's speed that he was soon switched from his customary centre position to the right wing, where he scored 44 tries during the 1960/61 campaign-second in the league's try-scoring charts to Tom Van Vollenhoven! By a bitter irony, the 'Flying Dentist' received a broken jaw while playing for Leeds and was later transferred to Hull. His spectacular touchdowns, in the style of former Saints' winger Steve Llewellyn, made him a real crowd pleaser!

In October 1959, full back Percy Landsberg became a Saint, for a £1,500 fee. A former Transvaal and Rhodesian representative, Landsberg held down a first team place for the opening months of the 1960/61 season and won a Lancashire Cup Winner's medal in Saints' 15-9 defeat of Swinton at Wigan on October 29th.1960. Before the new year, however, following a difference of opinion with the St.Helens Board, he had returned to South Africa. Landsberg was followed by Johnny Gaydon, a flying winger, who arrived at Knowsley Road in November 1960. Yet opportunities on the flanks were limited with the likes of Vollenhoven and Mick Sullivan around and he later carved out a successful career on the flanks with Widnes.

It was not until June 15th.1962 that the South African connection was resumed at Knowsley Road. Leonard Michael Anthony Killeen, from Uitenhage, Cape Province arrived in England to begin a spectacular career in the professional code. Originally a provincial representative as a full back in Rugby Union, he represented his country at basketball and also played first league baseball...a talented all-round sportsman! Killeen, who soon made the left wing position his own, was Saints' only other South African signing to reach anything like the heights of his good friend Tom Van Vollenhoven in Rugby League. Indeed, as a result of a serious injury to Kel Coslett at the start of the 1964/65 season, Lenny took over the place-kicking role that would add another dimension to his vast repertoire of skills. He remains the only player to top the league's goalkicking, try-scoring and overall points charts in the same season-Saints' fabulous four trophy campaign in 1965/66. Killeen shared top spot in the try-scorers with Wigan's Rhodesian winger Trevor Lake .

WHAT MIGHT HAVE BEEN!

Although Len Killeen was the Saints' last major South African signing, the Minutes of the St.Helens Board reveal that many more were linked with the club during the late 1950s, including centre Gert Pretorius, who later played for Workington Town and Gert Potgeiter, an international hurdler and Rugby Union threequarter. Yet one major signing that failed to materialise was much closer to home. Eric Ashton, the Great Britain centre, was placed on the transfer list by Wigan in January 1960. According to the Minutes of the St. Helens club for January 23rd: *"The Chairman said that the meeting had been called to decide what action to take should the £13,000 fee on Ashton be reduced by the League Management Committee on Sunday. A proposal to pay up to a figure £11,000 was defeated."* St.Helens supporters, who looked forward to the mouth-watering prospect of a Vollenhoven-Ashton link up were to be disappointed, as Ashton made his peace with the Central Park club. An opportunity missed, in retrospect.

The latter half of Tom's career at Knowsley Road was undoubtedly hindered by the lack of a long-standing centre partnership on the lines of that provided by Greenall and Large!

Some 34 years later, Eric has no doubts that the partnership would have flourished: *"Being St.Helens-born, I would have loved to have joined the Saints. I was always a winger's centre and I prided myself on the understanding I struck up with the man outside me. There is no doubt in my mind that Vol. and I would have done very well!"*

SPREADING THE GOSPEL

Despite the large number of South Africans turning professional with English clubs in the late Fifties and early Sixties, Rugby League was never able to establish a permanent toehold in the country, principally a result of intense pressure from the all-powerful Rugby Union lobby. The first move to establish the handling code was made in 1957, when the British and French World Cup squads played three matches against each other-at Durban, Benoni and East London-on their way home from the competition in Australia. Unfortunately, exhibition matches failed to arouse the interest of the South African sporting public and the promotion exercise was a failure.

The next serious attempts were made in 1961, when two organisations-Rugby League South Africa and The National League-were formed. Money appeared to be no object at first and several big-names from South African Rugby Union were induced to turn professional. In early January, 1962, rugby-mad St.Helens was reeling with the announcement that Tom Van Vollenhoven was wanted by those sponsoring the semi-professional game in South Africa and had received a cash offer. Ironically, the offer was made during the coldest temperatures that Tom and Leonie had endured in Britain. Leonie, in particular, was finding the British winters hard to bear!

"Vollenhoven of course, is under contract to Saints to play for them for the rest of his career," wrote Tom Ashcroft in the Reporter. *"If he played in the South African professional game, which owes no allegiance to the International Rugby League Body, St.Helens could make no legal claim to retain his services if he decided to go. Mr.Bill Fallowfield, the Rugby League Secretary told me yesterday that if clubs and leagues were formed in South Africa the development should be encouraged, but the question of affiliation or recognition would be a question for the International Rugby League Body."*

In the same article, Vollenhoven himself revealed that his loyalty to the Saints was as great as ever, but he had to look to the future when his playing days were over. *"I may only have 3 or 4 seasons left at the top,"* he continued. *"And what happens if I get a serious injury? My Physical Training Instructor's job at the Technical College is part-time and I do not get paid for holidays!"*

While newspaper telephone lines up and down the country buzzed with speculation about his future, and the story was re-told in the popular press with some alarming embellishments, Saints' Chairman Harry Cook and his Directors wasted no time in interviewing Tom to assure him where his future lay. The winters would get no milder, but much to the relief of thousands of St.Helens supporters, Tom turned the offer down-and scored a hat-trick in his next match, at home to Barrow for good measure! Yet he was still to play a part in promoting

McCormick's Men - 1962-63

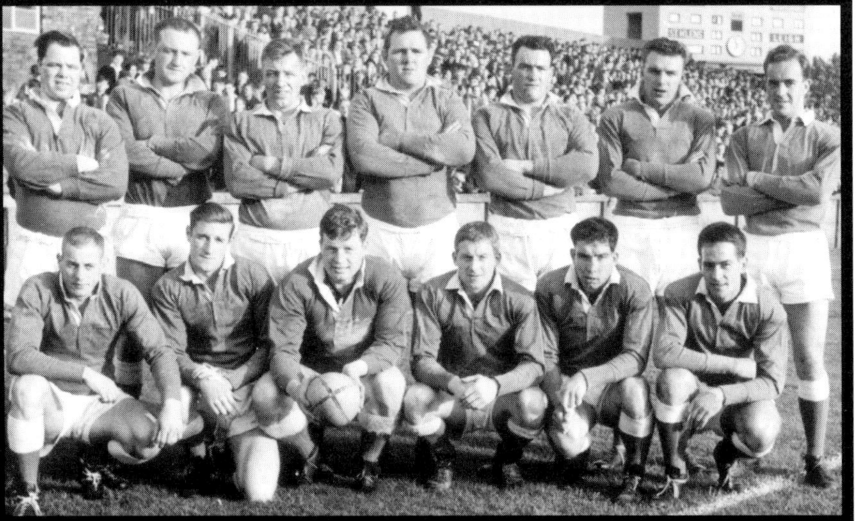

The Saints, in their change strip of blue jerseys, line up before the 21-3 victory over Leigh in the Western Division Championship at Knowsley Road, on August 22nd., 1962. No less than seven of the team were signed from Rugby Union.
Back Row L to R: FRED LEYLAND, prop forward. Ex-St.Helens R.U.F.C. forward who played over 50 matches for the Saints. A Policeman. RAY FRENCH, second row. Local-born former England Rugby Union international. Hard-grafting packman. Transferred to Widnes in 1967 as part of the deal that brought Frank Myler to Knowsley Road. BOB DAGNALL, hooker. Thatto-Heath born. Joined Saints from Rochdale Hornets in 1960. Great Britain international number nine. JOHN TEMBEY, second row. Renowned more as a ball-handling prop forward. Signed from Whitehaven in 1961. Cumberland and Great Britain representative. CLIFF WATSON, prop forward. Born in London's Mile End Road. Signed as a result of an intensive advertising campaign. Became Great Britain's most capped forward of all time. KEL COSLETT, Full back. Former Welsh Rugby Union international, making a successful home debut with six goals. Topped the goalkicking charts at the end of the season. Failed to score in only one match! KEITH NORTHEY, Stand off. Ex-West Park and Lancashire Rugby Union threequarter and the possessor of a devastating sidestep.
Front Row L to R: TOM VAN VOLLENHOVEN, right wing. Former South African international winger and the Saints' leading scorer during 1962/63 with 33 touchdowns. JOHN DONOVAN, left centre. Local product. A deceptive runner who later starred with Oldham. BILL MAJOR. Loose forward and Captain. Replacement for Vince Karalius. Joined Saints in a cash and exchange deal for Jim Measures. Retired prematurely as a result of work committments. ALAN BRIERS, Right centre. Fast and elusive threequarter who went on to Wembley glory with Widnes in 1964. WILF SMITH, scrum half. One of Saints' greatest utility backs, who enjoyed a well-deserved testimonial in 1967. Coached local amateur club Blackbrook with distinction. LEN KILLEEN, left wing. A sensational signing from South African Rugby Union also making a successful home debut, with a brace of tries. In 1966 became the only player to top the try-scorers and goalkickers' charts in the same season.

the game in his native country during the closed season!
In early May, 1962, representatives of the National Rugby League met with the Saints' Board to request that a St.Helens team, together with South African players from other English clubs, visit the Union and play five matches against local teams. There would be a guarantee given that no player would be approached with a view to signing for a South African club. At a special meeting of the St.Helens Board, on May 18th., matters were finally resolved:

"The Chairman introduced Mr.J.E.Gaushon, representative of the South African Rugby League, who had travelled from London to state a case following the invitation to St.Helens to tour South Africa for a period of three weeks. Mr.Gaushon gave a general picture of Rugby League in South Africa, it's formation and strength. He said that 77 players had been signed as professionals and that £16,000 had already been spent by the National League to launch the game. His body was prepared to spend an amount of £8-10,000 to finance the tour and would insure all players against injury or loss of ability to play. The English Rugby League had sanctioned the tour and permission had been sought to obtain guest players (South Africans) from Hull, Wigan and Wakefield. Any necessary guarantees against locating of players would be given. He summed up by saying should Rugby League be successful in South Africa, it would always be remembered that it was with the assistance of St.Helens. After Mr.Gaushon had retired from the meeting and following a full discussion, it was agreed by a majority vote not to accept the invitation, but permission was granted to Tom Van Vollenhoven to play in matches in South Africa."

Wakefield Trinity eventually accepted the South African invitation, despite being without the services of five players-Neil Fox, Poynton, Round, Turner and Wilkinson, who were touring Australia with the Great Britain squad. Yet interest was provided by their own South African contingent of Skene, Greenwood and Prinsloo, who formed an impressive threequarter line, which also included Tom Van Vollenhoven and Wigan full-back Fred Griffiths.

Despite a successful tour, against such teams as Bloemfontein Aquilae, Boksburg Vikings and the oddly named Vitnodiging Span, the ruthless opposition of South African Rugby Union interests took a heavy toll of the fledgling leagues. Grounds were difficult to obtain and players faced the threat of blacklisting by the Rugby Union authorities. The two leagues later combined, but it was too late. Gates dropped, financial backing dried up and a venture which had started with genuine enthusiasm ended in failure.

In September 1991, Tom, with his former Wigan adversary Trevor Lake, became involved in another attempt to try and introduce Rugby League into South Africa-this time on a purely amateur footing to enable players to enjoy a free gangway between the two codes. In January 1992, Tom and Trevor organised a Rugby League tournament in Pretoria-the first event of it's kind staged in South Africa for over 30 years! The major objective of establishing the 13-a-side code in a country where such phenomenal rugby talent exists was slowly beginning to take shape!

INTERNATIONAL WILDERNESS

Despite being regarded as one of the game's outstanding wingers in the early 'Sixties, the lack of international football was frustrating for Tom Van Vollenhoven, who had represented his country in the 15-a-side code at the highest level. Tom played four matches, of varying importance, for the Northern Rugby League XIII, as it became known. After a successful two try debut against France at the end of his first season as a professional, a 16,000 crowd packed into Knowsley Road for a repeat fixture on November 22nd., 1958. A feast of attacking rugby was in prospect. Vollenhoven formed a left-wing partnership with club colleague Duggie Greenall, while on the right was Warrington's brilliant Brian Bevan. Somewhat disappointingly, however, the match was a non-event. In a dour eighty minutes, the French pack dominated procedings to win by 26-8. Amazingly, Vollenhoven and Bevan were given few genuine running chances and failed to trouble the scorers. Yet the Van made one amazing, sidestepping run that beat six defenders. Unfortunately, Hunslet loose forward Shaw dropped Tom's pass with the line at his mercy!

A much sterner test was in store as Tom lined up with fellow South African Alan Skene in the centre against the 1961 New Zealand tourists at the now-demolished White City Stadium in Manchester. The Rugby League XIII emerged victorious by 22-20, with two Brian Bevan tries. Although Vollenhoven accepts that being South African-born ruled him out of top class international football, it is ironic that Bevan, the best Australian winger of his generation, should not have represented his country in the Test Match arena!

Tom's final representative appearance came at the Parc Des Princes, in Paris, on a Thursday night in October, 1961. This was an experimental game, against a French XIII, to test the viability of a new play-the-ball rule. The tackled player and tackler had to release the ball immediately and could take no further part in the game until the ball had been played by the hand or foot of another player. There was an all-South African backline in operation for the Rugby League XIII, Vollenhoven, his centre Skene and two other Wakefield players Greenwood and Prinsloo. Although Tom stole the show with an incredible 80 yard touchdown, the new rule did not find many supporters and the experiment was duly abandoned. The Australian Rugby League News described it as *"Scrappy and un-enterprising as any Rugby Union game can be. And this new idea virtually means the Union game played by thirteen men."*

In the close season of 1963, Tom was to miss the one South African attempt to enter international Rugby League, when a tour of Australia and New Zealand was arranged. The team was captained by forward Dawie Ackerman, who had played in Tom's debut Test Match against the British Lions in 1955 and contained several players with experience of the English game, such as Greenwood, Skene and Tom's former Saints' team-mate Johnny Gaydon. The tourists lost both 'Tests' against Australia, beating New Zealand 4-3 in Auckland. Unfortunately, rather than building on what had been achieved, interest in the 13-a-side code faded in South Africa once more.

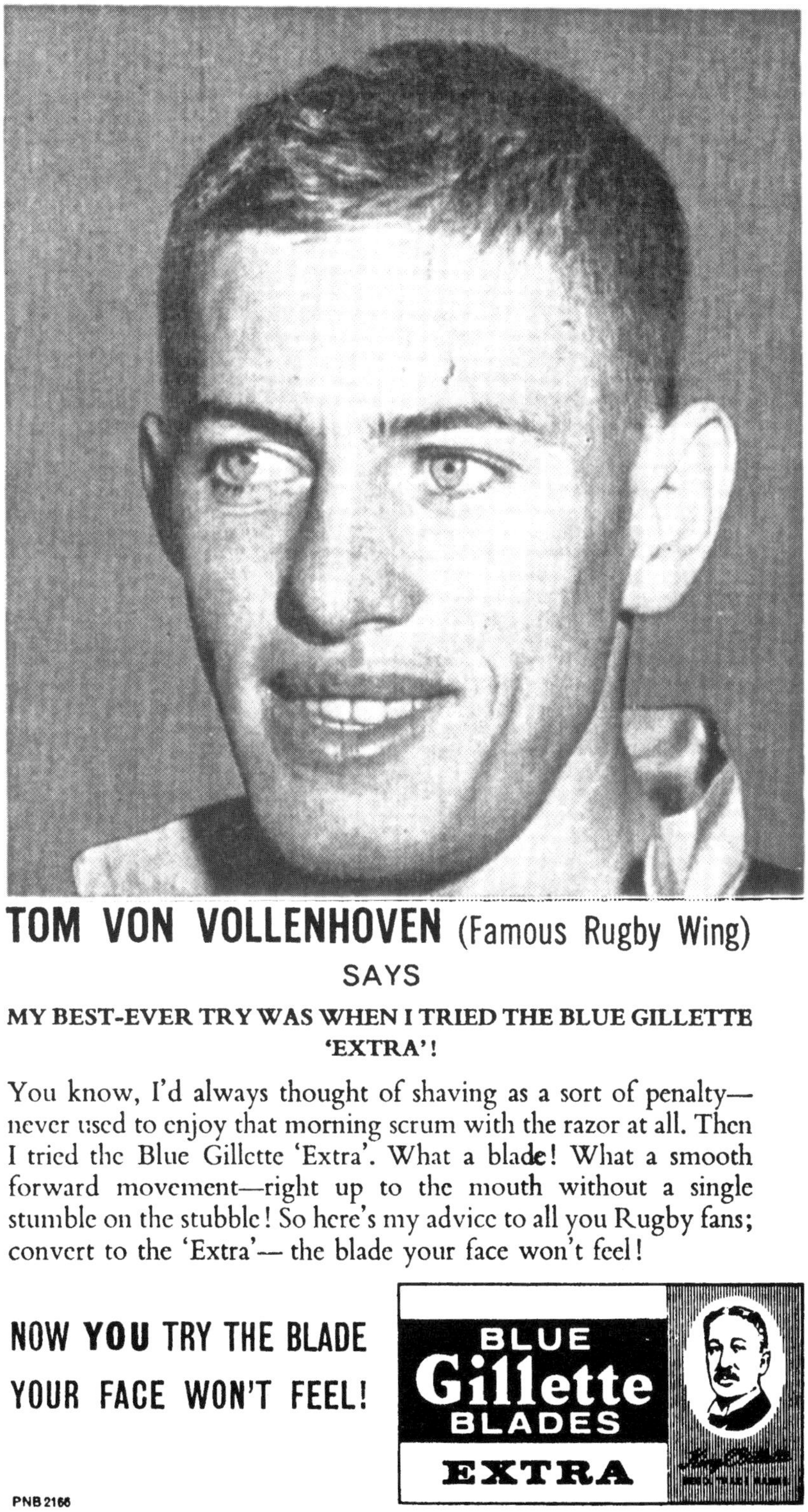
TOM VON VOLLENHOVEN (Famous Rugby Wing)
SAYS
MY BEST-EVER TRY WAS WHEN I TRIED THE BLUE GILLETTE 'EXTRA'!
You know, I'd always thought of shaving as a sort of penalty—never used to enjoy that morning scrum with the razor at all. Then I tried the Blue Gillette 'Extra'. What a blade! What a smooth forward movement—right up to the mouth without a single stumble on the stubble! So here's my advice to all you Rugby fans; convert to the 'Extra'— the blade your face won't feel!
NOW YOU TRY THE BLADE
YOUR FACE WON'T FEEL!
BLUE
Gillette
BLADES
EXTRA
PNB 2166

Advertisement featuring Tom Van Vollenhoven in the programme for Wakefield Trinity's South African Tour - Summer 1962. Ironically Tom's eldest son Keith was to feature in television commercials for the same company in the 1990s!

CHAPTER EIGHT

Winds of change

PICKING UP THE PIECES

Despite the Saints' spectacular Challenge Cup success in 1961, the Board of Directors were seemingly dissatisfied with the coaching position at the club. Alan Prescott's position had been tenuous for some time-Wembley had merely brought him a stay of execution. Indeed, during that particular season, the Directors offered former Leeds and Great Britain full back Jim Brough a temporary appointment to coach the backs before the cup ties. Fearing that such a move could signal the end for 'Precky,' a strong letter of protest was sent to the Board containing the signatures of 28 players-including Vollenhoven. This measure of the players' loyalty forced the Board to abandon their plans forthwith!
Before the 1961/62 season, however, the Board issued a 'job description' for the Coach:

1. *A selected panel of 18/20 players to train together as the First Team, with special sprinting instruction from Tom Van Vollenhoven .*

2. *Regular reports on injuries, Tuesday and Thursday evenings, with named reports of players not reporting for training.*

3. *The Coach to travel and return with the team to all away matches.*

4. *To be responsible for seeing that the players are on the coach following meals after away matches, also that in future, no specified time allowed for the players to have drinks.*

5. *To attend all 'A' team matches when not on duty with the first team.*

Needless to say, Tom proved to be the ideal role model for his team-mates, on the pitch as well as off, as he sprinted in for 14 tries in just 6 matches during September. The Saints faced Swinton in the Lancashire Cup Final at Central Park, Wigan, for the second successive season and once again Vollenhoven tormented the Lions' defence with one of St.Helens' five tries in a sparkling 25-9 triumph!

LANCASHIRE CUP FINAL
ST.HELENS 25 SWINTON 9
AT CENTRAL PARK, WIGAN
SATURDAY NOVEMBER 11TH. 1961

ST.HELENS Rhodes (try, 5 goals); Van Vollenhoven (try), Large (try), Mc.Ginn, Sullivan (try); Smith, Murphy (try); Leyland, Dagnall, Watson, French, Huddart, Karalius (Capt.)

SWINTON Gowers; Mc.Mahon, Fleet, Cummings, Speed; Parkinson, Cartwright; Thompson, T.Roberts, Bretherton (try), K.Roberts, Norburn, Blan (Capt. 3 goals).

Referee-Gelder (Wilmslow)
Attendance-30,000

Yet the county cup success was clouded by a remarkable slump in League fortunes, as the side nose-dived down the table losing five matches out of six in December. A shock home defeat by Oldham on

Lancashire Cup Winners 1961
Back row left to right, Fred Leyland, Dick Huddart, Bob Dagnall, Vince Karalius (Capt.), Cliff Watson, Ray French, Wilf Smith.
Front row left to right, Brian McGinn, Alex Murphy, Ken Large, Mick Sullivan, Austin Rhodes, Tom Van Vollenhoven.

December 16th. forced the St.Helens Directorate into a predictable and rather inevitable course of action by sacking Prescott. The Saints lay 15th. in the league table-a perilous position! A place in the top half of the league was essential at the end of 1961/62. For the first time in 50 years the two divisions system was to be re-introduced. The top 16 clubs were to form the First Division, the bottom 14, the Second, with two up and two down at the end of the season!

Prescott was finding it difficult to exert his discipline and deal with players who were, until recently, team-mates. The Wembley side was also in the throes of breaking up, with the loss of prop Ab Terry (to Leeds), second rower Don Vines (to Wakefield), and former skipper and loose forward Vince Karalius, who joined Widnes. Prescott's replacement was Stan Mc.Cormick, a former St.Helens and Warrington winger, who had been in charge of the 'A' team at Knowsley Road. Slowly but surely, Stan's insistence on higher standards of fitness, allied to fast, open rugby, pulled Saints out of the danger zone into 9th. position.

DAY OF INFAMY!

Life was never dull with Stan Mc.Cormick around and he recalls those early days at the helm with great relish: *"It was a pleasure to walk into the dressing room when it contained so many superb professionals like Vollenhoven, Huddart and Murphy. I used to say to them....'Listen, I'm the bloke who goes upstairs to the Boardroom on a Tuesday night and gets my whatnots chewed off!' I never got anything less than respect from the lads. With all due respect to all those who have gone since, I do believe that I was involved with the last great professionals at Knowsley Road! We had a great atmosphere at training. There was always banter. I was 44 and quite fit. I said to 'em once, during sprinting, 'I'll take yards for years!' Dick Huddart says 'I'll back Mc.Cormick!' I would be giving Vol. maybe 15-20 yards....but there were no takers!"*

Day of Infamy!
St.Helens 2 Huddersfield 13, Rugby League Challenge Cup, March 3rd 1962. Saints' trainer Norman Borrowdale applies the 'magic sponge' to a prostrate Tom Van Vollenhoven. Referee Eric Clay and his linesmen try to restore order, despite angry St.Helens players...and a lone spectator!
(John Huxley)

As the spectre of a possible Second Division place subsided during the second half of the 1961/62 campaign, hopes were high of retaining the Challenge Cup, especially when the Saints were drawn at home to Huddersfield in the second round of the competition. Although the Yorkshiremen were a formidable side-future League Champions in fact-the Saints had plundered a sensational 36-5 victory at Knowsley Road four weeks before, with Mick Sullivan notching five touchdowns against his former club and Vollenhoven chipping in with a brace.

Unfortunately, Saints' hopes of a Wembley return were dashed as early as the 20th. minute. Already 7-0 ahead, Huddersfield were pressing on the St.Helens right flank when Tom Plucked the ball out of the air for a superb opportunist interception and cut inside from the touchline. Ramsden, the visitors' loose forward, was caught off-balance by Vol's change of direction and lunged, despairingly with arm outstretched. Tom copped a real 'bell-ringer' and dropped like a stone to the turf, with Ramsden finishing prostrate behind him. Referee Eric 'Sergeant Major' Clay's whistle blew, his finger pointed to the dressing rooms and Ramsden started the long walk to the accompaniment of a cacophany of booing from the enraged St.Helens Popular Side. *"I don't know where Ramsden came from,"* recalls Tom, *"I didn't even feel the shot - I was out cold long before I hit the deck!"*

Yet worse was to come as the din was punctuated by a momentary stunned silence as scrum half Murphy trailed a few yards behind the Huddersfield man. Pandemonium was about to ensue! Players of both sides gathered round Eric Clay voicing their protests. The crowd hurled snowballs onto the pitch and one spectator promptly vaulted the boundary wall to aim one such missile at Mr.Clay before returning hurridly to the relative safety of the terraces as Police Officers rushed in. A disgruntled Murphy joined Ramsden for the early bath and to quote Tom Ashcroft in the Reporter, Saints with Vollenhoven stunned and Murphy dismissed were like 'A gun without a bullet' as the Yorkshiremen coasted to a 13-2 victory. The Fartowners eventually reached the final, where they were beaten 12-6 by rivals Wakefield Trinity.

According to Stan Mc.Cormick, Murphy and Clay were traditional antagonists: *"I said to Eric before the match 'You know what a volatile lad Alex is.' He replied gruffly...'He gets same chance as everyone else!' Anyhow, Ramsden flattens Vol. and Alex runs 30 yards to get involved. Ramsden had no chance of stopping Vol.-he just stuck his arm out. God knows what the punishment would be for that to day....probably three years in Walton Jail! Mind you, Tom was a hard man in his own right. I remember on the Monday Tom and I were back at the club being interviewed by Franklin Engleman for his 'Down Your Way' programme. He asked us about the cup-tie and played some records. I think my choice was Shirley Bassey.....!"*

RUNNING FREE!

In a newspaper article of the early Sixties, Tom spoke of the sheer impossibility of trying to smash one long-standing Rugby League record-that of 80 tries in a season, set by Huddersfield's Australian winger Albi Rosenfeld in 1913/14. *"I'm willing to settle for this: I am all-out to beat Brian Bevan's 72 tries in a season post-war record,"* he concluded. *"If I can do that I will be more than satisfied!"* Despite topping the try-scoring charts for three consecutive seasons, however, Tom's highest total of 62, in Saints' free-scoring 1958/59 campaign, failed to threaten the Warrington Flyer's record.

Tom holds the career and seasonal try-scoring records at St.Helens, yet was unable to break the individual record of six touchdowns in a match. In the 1961/62 season, he came closest to achieving this feat, against Blackpool Borough at Knowsley Road, when the Saints recorded a comfortable 37-5 success. Tom, partnered at centre by local lad Alan Briers, used all his speed and elusiveness to notch a hat-trick in the first half. When he scored a fourth immediately after the restart, the crowd were warming to the prospect of a possible record-breaking performance! Two more scintillating touchdowns within two minutes of each other-with ten minutes remaining-and the crowd were screaming for the Saints to get Tom on the move once more!

Although Tom strained every sinew to oblige the fans, Blackpool were not prepared to cooperate in the establishment of records! The visiting defenders blocked Tom's supply of possession by taking Briers in a series of man-and-ball tackles. Yet Vol. could only have been inches over the touchline as he charged over in the corner with a couple of minutes remaining-but it was not to be!

Tom was beaten into second place in the League's try-scoring charts by his great rival Billy Boston at the end of 1961/62. Ironically, in an end of season friendly against S.H.A.P.E. Indians, a team of American Servicemen from N.A.T.O. Headquarters in Paris, Tom scored seven tries for the Saints. Although Tom's display added considerably to the entertainment value for the

Got any Shirley Bassey?
Saints' coach Stan McCormick is interviewed by Franklin Engleman for his 'Down Your Way' programme. Tom Van Vollenhoven looks on approvingly! (Stan McCormick)

10,000 crowd at Knowsley Road, scoring feats in exhibition matches do not count in the compilation of records!

THE TOAST IS...SUCCESS!

By January 1962, Tom had relinquished his post as Physical Training Instructor at the newly-opened St.Helens Technical College and intimated that he would like to enter the licensed trade-hardly an unusual occupation for rugby players-past and present! Several months later, Tom was installed as Mine Host in the Ring O'Bells Hotel-a typical 'old-fashioned' hostelry on the corner of Westfield Street and Eccleston Street, on the outskirts of St.Helens Town Centre. Although Tom's tenancy at the now-demolished watering hole was to last barely nine months, his presence behind the bar meant that it became a popular meeting place for St.Helens fans who wanted to talk about goings on at Knowsley Road 'first-hand!'

Like most of his team-mates, Tom was not averse to a drink or two. Not the usual pint of bitter, mild or lager, however. Peter Harvey explains that Tom's unusual preference once brought him into conflict with Saints' Chairman Harry Cook: *"Tom was 'raised' on peach brandy and was essentially a shorts drinker. When we went away we were a very professional side. If the club said you could have one drink after the match, that's exactly what they meant! I remember I was with Tom over in Yorkshire and we were having our meal. Most of us ordered shandies, or in Cliff Watson's case, a pint of orange. Tom ordered a brandy. The waiter said that he had been told not to serve spirits to the players. Tom offered to pay for it himself. So the waiter brought him a brandy and Chairman Harry Cook came over to our table. 'Come on Tom,' says Harry. 'You know the rules about spirits after the match.' Tom argued that he drank spirits anyway. 'What's the difference if I have a brandy now, or ten when I get back home?' Harry didn't like the idea of anyone seeing him drinking it-especially the younger players in the side!"*

THE LION BITES BACK!

The prospect of facing Tom Van Vollenhoven-with or without the ball-was enough to give even the most capable of wingers sleepless nights! The Flying Springbok's range of attacking skills made him virtually impossible to shackle on a man-to-man basis. Opposing wingers faced further frustration when they tried to get past him, courtesy of Tom's scrooge-like defensive qualities! Indeed, it was considered an achievement to score a try against him. Few have managed to do it twice in a match. Yet even the greatest players have a 'bogey'-someone who has given them particular trouble during their career. In Tom Van Vollenhoven's case, it was the Swinton and Great Britain winger John Stopford-the only man to score a hat-trick against him, a feat he achieved on two occasions!

A strong, determined runner, Stopford registered his first hat-trick against Vollenhoven in a league match at Station Road, Swinton, on April 18th.1959, when the Lions recorded a 19-11 success. No doubt buoyed by his achievement, the Wigan-born flyer scorched in for three more touchdowns seven days later at Castleford! *"Despite those three tries, Saints became a bit of a bogey team for Swinton in the early Sixties,"* recalls John. *"We played three Lancashire Cup Finals against them in succession and lost the lot! Unfortunately, I missed every one through injury-a bitter disappointment! The two greatest wingers I faced during my career were Boston and Vollenhoven. Billy was the more adaptable of the two-he could play stand-off, centre and full back as well as wing. Yet Tom would give me nightmares with his pace! Give him an inch and he would leave you for dead. He was a great sportsman and we remain good friends to this day. I remember in March 1962, when they picked the Great Britain Touring team. I was out at the time with shoulder problems. In his regular column in a local newspaper, Tom said that the best left-winger had been left behind! At least I managed to be selected for the 1966 tour!"*

Swinton certainly missed Stopford in the third successive meeting of the Saints and Lions at Central Park on 27th.October 1962. In the 11th.minute Ken Roberts, the Swinton prop slung out a wild pass which was brilliantly intercepted by Vollenhoven who streaked 40 yards to the line. The try was converted by Saints' former Welsh international full back Kel Coslett, who added a penalty goal shortly afterwards to give the Red and Whites a crucial seven point lead. Despite a tremendous second half rally, in which Lions' skipper Albert Blan added two goals, the Saints' defence held firm. Although Vollenhoven's smash and grab score sealed the match for St.Helens, Albert Blan's decision to play against the wind and driving rain in the first half was considered to be a crucial error of judgement by the critics.

LANCASHIRE CUP FINAL
ST.HELENS 7 SWINTON 4
AT CENTRAL PARK, WIGAN
SATURDAY 27TH.OCTOBER, 1962

ST.HELENS Coslett (2 goals); Van Vollenhoven (try), Donovan, Smith, Sullivan; Benyon, Heaton; Arkwright, Dagnall, Watson, Tembey, Huddart, Major (Capt.).

SWINTON Gowers; Mc.Mahon, Halliwell, Buckley, Speed;

Parkinson, Cartwright; K.Roberts, T.Roberts, Morgan, Norburn, Bonser, Blan (Capt. 2 goals)

Referee-Coates (Pudsey)
Attendance-23,523
Receipts- £4,122

CATCH US IF YOU CAN!

Later in a season ravaged by the Big Freeze for almost four months, Swinton and Stan Mc.Cormick's rejuvenated St.Helens side became locked in a race for the First Division title. On March 16th., however, Widnes topped the table with 24 points from 15 matches. Swinton, in 11th. position drew with Hull and looked anything like genuine contenders! Yet the Lions began a glorious run of 17 successive victories to snatch the title in sensational style-winding up with a last match victory against Widnes, who finished behind St.Helens on points average. *"We were not exactly a big side, but we threw the ball about and things just seemed to click,"* remembers John Stopford.

No-one could dispute Swinton's right to be champions after an Easter double against the Saints, who were making their own determined bid to overhaul Widnes. The Lions scraped a 9-8 success at home on Easter Saturday and took on their rivals two days later in the pressure-cooker atmosphere of a near 20,000 crowd at Knowsley Road. The scores were locked at 7-7 until early in the second half when Stopford kicked a loose ball past Saints' full back Coslett on half-way and surged past him to score by the posts. As St.Helens fans looked on in disbelief, Swinton were soon celebrating a second touchdown. Second rower Cummings made a telling break before the ball fizzed out to Stopford for number two. Saints' last hopes of salvaging the match-and their title hopes-disappeared with a typical piece of magic from Swinton's skipper Albert Blan. A brilliant wide pass to Stopford saw the completion of a sensational hat-trick and a much-needed 24-9 success.

Much to the chagrin of Tom Van Vollenhoven and the Saints, it later transpired that Stopford should not even have taken the field : *"I was not down to play that day,"* he recalls. *"I was under treatment for a back injury. I went to an osteopath in Manchester during the week and he diagnosed a twisted pelvis. He told me to come back the following Monday and not to play against the Saints. But we had several cry-offs and they got me onto the field after a good rub down. I scored three tries against Tom, but that was just good fortune on the day.....Tom was the best winger I ever clapped my eyes on! Everyone has a 'bogey'.....mine was the Workington and Salford full-back Sid Lowden. I could never go past him-he seemed to have me in his pocket every time!"*

Saints' Coach Stan Mc.Cormick has vivid recollections of that title shoot-out, and Stopford's fellow international centre Alan Buckley: *"I said to Tom 'Don't get drawn in to Buckley at any price!' It was right in front of me on the bench. I saw Tommy going in-as s oon as he took one step I knew what was going to happen. Buckley fed Stopford and that was that. Back in the dressing room Tommy says 'I'm sorry Stan, I've learned something today!' It all happened in a split second, but we all make mistakes. Buckley gave Stopford great service, just like Albert Pimblett did to Brian Bevan at Warrington. Don't forget that Swinton were also a great tactical team."*

GLORY IN THE CENTRE SPOT!

In the Autumn of 1963, America was on the verge of a 'pop' invasion by British groups such as The Beatles, Rolling Stones and The Dave Clark Five. There was an invasion of a different kind at St.Helens R.L.F.C., however-an influx of Rugby Union talent-as team building continued at a fast pace. Former Llanelli full-back Kel Coslett looked forward to retaining his spot at the top of the goalkicking charts, while Cen Williams (Cardiff), Peter Harvey (Liverpool), and Welsh international second rower John Warlow were added to the first team panel. Indeed, it was not unusual for the Saints to field a complete back division of former Rugby Union players.

Such was the case as the side reached it's fourth successive Lancashire Cup Final on October 26th.1963. This time their opponents were Second Division Leigh-ironically the Saints had beaten long-standing rivals Swinton in the first round at Station Road! There were some significant changes for the big match. Coslett was an automatic choice at full back and former Birkenhead Park centre Keith Northey partnered Harvey on the left flank. As a result of injuries, however, Len Killeen took up the right wing berth, with Tom Van Vollenhoven in the centre. Although Tom had appeared in the centre once before, without much success, the switch was welcomed by Tom Ashcroft in the Reporter: *"Vollenhoven has not been getting the best of service over the last few months.....he has been looking for his chances in the middle so much of late that he will be of greater scoring potential in the centre."*

Gallant Leigh fought hard and held a 4-0 lead until the Saints snatched the advantage with a Coslett penalty and a Killeen try just before half time. Vollenhoven showed great awareness by hanging back in the line to allow Wilf Smith's cut-out pass to send Killeen in at the corner for a superb touchdown. It was stand off half Smith who provided Vollenhoven with his now customary County Cup Final try shortly afterwards. His grubber kick was mis-fielded by Leigh left winger Leadbetter. The ball squirted out and Vollenhoven, with a lightening pick-up, flung himself over an attempted tackle to make the touchdown. A well-deserved try by Smith himself sealed a 15-4 success for the Saints. The critics were unanimous in their praise of Vollenhoven the centre threequarter, typifed by Tom Ashcroft: *"He blotted out Collins, Leigh's young hope and struck up a close link with Killeen early on in the game. I do not think it would be fair or wise to regard Tom as a permanent inside man, but as a temporary expedient, Stan Mc.Cormick could not have done better for a cup final."*

LANCASHIRE CUP FINAL
ST.HELENS 15 LEIGH 4

AT STATION ROAD, SWINTON
SATURDAY, OCTOBER 26TH.1963

ST.HELENS Coslett (3 goals); Killeen (try), Van Vollenhoven (try), Northey, Harvey; Smith (try), Murphy; Tembey, Dagnall, Watson, French, Ashcroft, Major (Capt.).

LEIGH Risman; Tyrer (2 goals), G.Lewis, Collins, Leadbetter; Rhodes, Entwhistle; Robinson, J.Lewis, Owen, Murphy, Martyn, Hurt.
Referee-Gelder (Wilmslow)

The Great Outsider!
Tom is shackled by the Castleford defence during the 6-3 Challenge Cup defeat at Knowsley Road on February 8th 1964.
Centre Bryan Todd is next to Tom.
(St.Helens Reporter)

THE GREAT OUTSIDER

During the 1963/64 season, Tom Van Vollenhoven scored just 22 tries in 35 matches-his lowest total since joining the professional ranks in 1957. It was the first time that Tom had not led the Saints' try-scorers outright, sharing the spoils with Peter Harvey. His centre partners were chopped and changed with regularity and Vol. was not happy with his lot at Knowsley Road. In January 1964, he announced-not for the first time-that he would return to South Africa at the end of the campaign. A clear source of his dissatisfaction was that the Saints had become over-reliant upon down-the-middle forward tactics. Chances for the threequarters were at a premium. This was highlighted after a home defeat at the hands of a skilful Castleford side in the first round of the Challenge Cup at Knowsley Road. Tom Ashcroft in the Reporter summed up the situation in his usual succinct manner: *"No passes out of the tackle, no forwards supporting the man with the ball, no constructive ideas......Castleford, a snappy lot of ball-handlers had the opposition taped in various ways. It was no coincidence that Vollenhoven's strip was nearly as clean as it was at the start, for once again he had played the role of the Great Outsider."*

It was a difficult time for the Flying Springbok with such a dearth of good quality ball. As Peter Harvey explains, it is always about demanding the ball: *"There are certain players in the side who control the game because they demand the football...they get first option on what happens. At the Saints, Alex Murphy demanded the ball and had first option on what happened. Needless to say Alex used to love taking on the opposition. To that extent, Murphy controlled his own destiny more than Tom who was dependent upon the ball getting to him!"*

A HARD DAYS NIGHT!

Stan Mc.Cormick and the St.Helens Board made positive steps to introduce a ball-handler into the forwards by the blooding of loose forward Doug Laughton and the signing of the veteran Welsh prop forward Stan Owen from Leigh, who went on to captain the side. Although the Saints had finished in third place in the First Division behind Champions Swinton and Wigan, there was a chance of glory in the Western Division Final. This competition replaced the county leagues and each club played four other clubs home and away. St.Helens had qualified for the Final against Swinton at Central Park, Wigan on May 16th.1964.

Tom Van Vollenhoven had missed the preceding five matches as a result of a troublesome knee injury, but was recalled to the side, principally to try and shackle the Lions' danger man John Stopford-the League's leading try-scorer. Tom managed to stop the Swinton flyer on several occasions when danger threatened, yet there was nothing he could do to prevent Stopford scoring a try to level the scores at 7-7 after half time. Less than five minutes remained when Murphy broke through and slipped the ball to second-rower Warlow. Tembey continued the move and sent a perfectly-timed pass to the supporting Ray French, who stepped out of Parkinson's tackle and galloped 15 yards to plunge over the line.

As Tom and his team-mates went up to collect their medals, they looked round to see their Coach being carried away from the trainers' dugout with his face covered in blood. Poor Stan Mc.Cormick had leapt up in the air in jubilation after the winning try and forgot about the concrete roof! Returning from the final league fixture at Castleford less than a week later, Stan received a more serious blow to his pride: *"I was sat near the back of the bus next to Stan Owen...and he says 'I think you're a good coach. I understand what you are on about.' Shortly after, Harry Cook beckons me to come to the front of the bus and tells me that my contract is not going to be renewed. I said 'You mean I'm sacked?' He says 'No...we are not renewing your contract.' He tells me to this day that I wasn't sacked-but I wasn't there the season after! So I went back to Stan and he asks me what's wrong. I said 'You know what you were saying about me being a good coach? Well they've sacked me!' Stan replied 'At least there's one thing....they haven't sacked you on an empty stomach!' He had a point, I suppose!"*

Although the rather undignified manner of his dismissal reflected the ruthless nature of professional sport, a top club like St.Helens demanded league titles and Challenge Cups, which Stan had failed to deliver, despite being successful in his own right. At least Tom Van Vollenhoven was to remain a St.Helens player for the start of the 1964/65 campaign.

Yet the days when Tom could quite justifiably claim to be the game's number one wing threequarter were coming to an end.

Almost There!
Tom crashes over to complete a stunning hat-trick as a centre in the 19-8 victory over Warrington in the League match at Knowsley Road on November 2nd. 1963. Making an unsuccessful last ditch tackle is Warrington scrum half Jackie Edwards, whose son Shaun, found fame with Wigan and Great Britain some years later!
(St.Helens Reporter)

CHAPTER NINE

Turmoil and Recovery

KNEE DEEP IN THE BLUES!

There were raised eyebrows amongst St.Helens fans with the appointment of a relatively unknown figure, Joe Coan, as Coach for the 1964/65 season. A rugby union coach back in his native Cumberland, Coan had little pedigree to speak of in the professional code.Yet he was no stranger to the Knowsley Road scene. A local Physical Training Teacher, Coan had taken the Saints for indoor training at Rivington High School during the Great Freeze of 1962/63 and continued fitness work with the players under Stan Mc.Cormick. He was keen to take the job when Mc.Cormick's contract was not renewed at the end of the 1963/64 campaign. Physical fitness was his main priority and he was able to apply training techniques from other sports such as swimming-a particular interest of his-with spectacular success.

The 'Super-Fit' Saints, under the captaincy of Alex Murphy, made a remarkable start to the season, with 21 straight wins including a 12-4 Lancashire Cup Final victory over seemingly perenial opponents Swinton! Yet for the first time there was no Tom Van Vollenhoven in the Saints' line-up. Indeed, Tom's fitness had been in question even before the start of the season. Seven years of top-class Rugby League-as very much a marked man-were taking their inevitable toll on the Flying Springbok. Tom recalls that his rugby career was in jeopardy: *"I ended up having two cartilage operations. Jimmy Heron, the surgeon, took the outside cartilage out on my left knee. In my first game back I felt this pain again. Murphy kicked through and I jumped for the ball. My opponent tackled me while I was in the air and I felt this pain. I went back to Heron and he said that the inside cartilage had gone. I said to Heron 'Well, I'll stop playing.' The operation on the outside cartilage was extremely painful. These days it's just like pulling a tooth! I said to him , 'No, I won't have the 'op', I'll pack it in.' He says, 'Well, you can pack it in, but you have got to have the operation, otherwise your knee will be stiff when you get older.' Now, I didn't want a stiff knee, so I had the second operation. I still played for several seasons afterwards!"*

According to the St.Helens Reporter for 29th.September, 1964, Tom could call on extra family support to aid his recuperation: *"The parents of Tom Van Vollenhoven, Mr. and Mrs.Peter Van Vollenhoven, of Waverley, Pretoria, who have been spending a holiday in St.Helens should be able to see their footballing son over his cartilage operation before they return. Tom goes into hospital today for treatment on Thursday. Tom's six year old daughter has been in the same hospital since Sunday for observation. She has had a minor breathing difficulty."*

Apart from the loss of his star winger, there were further problems for Coach Coan, however, when regular full-back Kel Coslett broke his ankle against Rochdale in August. Frankie Barrow stepped into the number one jersey with great aplomb, while Coan plumped for Len Killeen to take over the kicking role. After an uncertain start, the South African with a kick like a mule found length and direction with a vengeance. His season's total of 141 was beaten only by Hull K.R. full back Cyril Kellett with 150.

Killeen's 26 tries meant that he led the overall points scorers with 360, comfortably beating Kellett himself (306) and the great Neil Fox of Wakefield (281). In what was an uncertain time for Tom Van Vollenhoven, his South African team-mate was proving to be very much a key figure in the side's chase for honours during 1964/65.

THE COMEBACK TRAIL

Tom's road back to fitness began on a rain-soaked afternoon in the 'A' team at Knowsley Road against Salford in mid-December. On what was described as the wettest weekend for several years, only a few hundred brave spectators huddled under the Main and Popular Side stands-despite the return of the Flying Springbok! Understandably, Vol. had no great part to play in the Saints' hard-won 8-7 victory. Most important of all-he had come through 80 minutes of rugby unscathed. The saturated pitch made footholds precarious and there could have been no greater stress on the troublesome knee than those imposed by the twists and turns in such difficult conditions. The Salford team showed no respect for reputations and Tom received his usual quota of double tackles. Yet, as Tom Ashcroft wrote after the match: *"Vollenhoven was wisely not in the mood for heroics. I feel confident that he will show he is far from a back number when he has tuned up to match fitness and there are vital deeds to be done."*

CRISIS OF CONFIDENCE

Tom Van Vollenhoven returned to first team duty against Whitehaven at Knowsley Road on January 23rd., 1965-after almost four months on the sidelines-and scored two tries in the Saints' comfortable 16-3 success. Yet it was not simply a case of regaining match fitness for the South African Flyer. The tries simply would not come and this clearly had a marked effect on Tom's confidence. After the home match against Huddersfield in late February, a convincing six-try performance with Vol. once again drawing a blank, the situation was highlighted by Tom Ashcroft in the Reporter: *"What the spectators did not get was a return to form by Vollenhoven, who has been on the fringe of things since his return from injury. This time it was not a case of the ball never going his way, but a question of the South African being unable to accept chances that he would have swallowed up in his best days. Vollenhoven's injuries have not only cost him speed and poise, but skill in taking the final pass-and that is something I just cannot understand.........Saints could have done done more than they have to smooth Vollenhoven's return. This is a vital matter, for I am among those who refuse to write off the South African and consider that he will recover when he gets a clean service. The greatest need is for an outside back who can size up an attacking situation so quickly that the decision he makes has the leisurely air-and his pass or kick is all the more accurate for being unhurried....an attribute Duggie Greenall certainly possessed."*

St.Helens Directors would doubtless continue to rue the day they chose not to bring Wigan's Eric Ashton to Knowsley Road. The tall Great Britain centre still formed a formidable partnership with his winger, Billy Boston! The chopping and changing of Tom's centre partners was also a factor-with Keith Northey, Tony Barrow and Cen Williams sharing the number three jersey during matches in February and early March.

After the home defeat against the 'Old Enemy' Wigan, on March 23rd.-the side who had knocked St.Helens out of the Challenge Cup at Central Park several weeks before-Tom suffered the ultimate indignity of being dropped for the first and only time in his career. *"Tom has suffered for want of a regular top class centre and a fast service,"* wrote Tom Ashcroft. *"But in Tuesday's game against Wigan he was given far more opportunities than usual and was unable to make the most of several half chances. For that reason he has gone back to the 'A' Team ....In my view he has not fully recovered his old physical and mental snap. He can never be the flyer he was and his future depends on his ability to get tuned up again. If he accepts the challenge, he could still be of service to a team that is not well off for experienced backs."*

Tom's place in the First Team to play Salford at the Willows was taken by Tom Pimblett, a local lad who had deputised for him during his cartilage operations earlier in the campaign with great success. *"Vol. wasn't exactly pleased about it,"* recalls Pimblett. *"It was very much a bitter-sweet occasion for me! As a schoolboy I used to go to Knowsley Road and my idols were Frank Carlton and Steve Llewellyn, both great wingers-and then Vollenhoven arrived and he simply topped the lot! I remember that both the First and 'A' teams played at Salford that afternoon. We watched the 'A' team lads before our match-which we lost 8-11!"*

Ironically, the 'A' team enjoyed an easy 30-0 victory, although Vollenhoven did not get much chance to show his paces. The trialist winger on the other flank-Dave Leatherbarrow-notched an impressive hat-trick!

St.Helens 'A' versus Salford 'A' 27th.March 1965: Coslett; Van Vollenhoven, Northey, J.Smith, D.Leatherbarrow; Kelly, Jones; Ward, Burdell, Donegan, Warlow, Markey, Egan. Subs-Gartland, Marsden.

"I didn't keep my place," recalls Tom Pimblett ruefully. *"Vol. was back for the next match, against Hull K.R. and I was on the bench. Mind you, I won three medals during the season-Lancashire Cup, Lancashire League and League League Leaders-so things could have been much worse! The pack was the mainstay of the side-the fittest in the game under Joe Coan-and play tended to be down the middle, perhaps to the detriment of the men out wide!"*

The 'A' team game at the Willows proved to be a significant watershed in what had been such a frustrating season for Tom Van Vollenhoven. Just turned thirty and virtually written off by many St.Helens supporters, he bounced back with a vengeance as the Saints embarked upon the Top 16 Play-Offs. Tom scored in all three rounds of the competition as they prepared to meet Halifax in the Final at Station Road, Swinton. Unfortunately, the newly-established partnership with Cen Williams, that had produced 9 tries in 10 matches for Vollenhoven, was broken when the Welshman was declared unfit for the big match. Tom was switched into the centre, with Peter Harvey wearing the coveted number two jersey.

As fate would have it, there was to be disappointment at the final hurdle for Vollenhoven. The Yorkshire side, who finished in 7th. place in the league table, scored the all-important first try through

Skipper and right centre John Burnett in the 26th.minute and never lost the lead. The Saints suffered a blow when ace ball-distributor John Tembey was forced to leave the field just before half time. Worse was to follow as Burnett scored his second try at another vital stage of the game in the second half when only a point separated the teams. Halifax, workmanlike and efficient, thoroughly deserved their 15-7 victory. St.Helens lost far too much possession to put the Yorkshiremen under any kind of sustained pressure. Although Killeen scored Saints' only try from the left flank, there were few chances for the backs to shine!

Determined to make up for lost time, Tom trained hard during the Summer on a local athletics track, often accompanied by Tom Pimblett. Indeed, Vollenhoven's experience in the threequarter line was to become a vital factor during the 1965/66 season-when the Saints were to hit the silver trail with a vengeance once more!

CHAMPIONSHIP FINAL
ST.HELENS 7 HALIFAX 15
AT STATION ROAD, SWINTON
SATURDAY 22ND.MAY 1965

ST.HELENS F.Barrow; Harvey, Vollenhoven, Northey, Killeen (try, 2 goals); Murphy (Capt.), Smith; Tembey, Dagnall, Watson, French, Mantle, Laughton.

HALIFAX James (3 goals); Jackson (try), Burnett (Capt. 2 tries), Kellett, Freeman; Robinson, Daley; Roberts, Harrison, Scroby, Fogerty, Dixon, Renilson.

Referee-Brown (Dewsbury)
Attendance-20,776
Receipts- £6,141
Harry Sunderland Trophy-
Fogerty (Halifax)

THE SUPER FIT SAINTS

Saints' Coach Joe Coan was a hard task-master during the twice-weekly sessions on the Knowsley Road training pitch during 1965/66-a major factor in the side's success at the end of the campaign. Tom was never the most enthusiastic of trainers, however, and made his views known in a rugby league annual of the early 'Sixties: *".....the unfortunate part of training today is that the methods are outdated and exceedingly boring........What happens at present is that the first few minutes of the hour-long period on Tuesdays and Thursdays is used to warm up the players with a few laps of the ground. This is generally followed with the usual routine pattern of an exercise period, coaching session and finally a period when the new ideas and movements-of which there seem to be few-are put into operation......when I first came over here to play for St.Helens I really looked forward to my training sessions because I really enjoyed myself. But now the same monotonous routine week in week out has killed all the pleasure I once had! I think that all the gym equipment should be brought into use in an effort to break the dreadfully monotonous routine we are suffering at the moment."*

Clearly, Tom would welcome the variety of methods and situations used by the modern-day St.Helens coaching team to make training more interesting-and meaningful! *"It is true that Tom was never the greatest trainer in the world,"* recalls Peter Harvey. *"In this respect, it is interesting to compare Tom and Alex Murphy, who was the Captain of the side at the time. Murphy was always very keen and always out there in front-a good role model! Yet this fellow Coan was a sadist! If you dropped out he would say 'Can't train, can't play!' You just had to hang on in there. There were quite a number of times that you went over the hedge to be sick. Everyone hated Joe at that moment-give us a knife*

Reeling in the years!
Tom leaves a trail of bemused Castleford defenders in his wake to score in the Saints' 21-6 league success at Knowsley Road on 18th September 1965 - one of his 18 touchdowns during the four cups campaign of 1965-66.
(St.Helens Reporter)

and we would have killed him on the spot-but he would just laugh and say 'Okay.... so you've been sick.... c'mon ...let's go and do some more!' It was this level of intensity that really made us a special team!"

MARCHING ON THE SILVER TRAIL

Joe Coan's super-fit Saints began the season with a 15-4 home success against Champions Halifax and embarked upon a tremendous unbeaten run of 19 league matches, ending with defeat at Oldham on January 8th. Only Wakefield, Wigan and Swinton-who recorded a creditable double-lowered the Saints' colours as the team retained both the League Leader's Trophy and the Lancashire League title. Yet there were disappointments in the first half of the campaign. Rivals Swinton broke their hoodoo with a shock 7-8 success at Knowsley Road in the first round of the Lancashire Cup. Thus St.Helens' 20 match unbeaten run in the competition, stretching back to the infamous 'Bevan' final of 1959 had come to an end! Although Tom Van Vollenhoven proved he still had the ability to produce the goods when it mattered, including a magnificent five-try spree at home to Workington, it was his partner on the other flank-Len Killeen-who was grabbing the headlines. The South African Flyer led both the try-scoring and goal-kicking charts at the end of the season-a record in itself-while his incredible 336 point haul represented almost 45% of his team's total in league and cup matches. Len's phenomenal touch escaped him only once, in the Final of the inaugural B.B.C.2 Floodlit Trophy against Castleford at Knowsley Road in December, when he failed with a number of penalty attempts he would have normally converted with ease. Castleford won 4-0 and deprived Tom Van Vollenhoven of the only winner's medal missing from his collection!

SUCCESS ON A PLATE

Strength in depth-and the addition of several key players to the squad in the New Year-were the major factors in the Saints' success during the 1965/66 campaign. On the eve of the cup deadline in the New Year, veteran hooker Bill Sayer joined St.Helens from rivals Wigan for a bargain £1,000, together with Albert Halsall, a mobile prop forward from Salford. The re-shaped front row, which also included the mighty Cliff Watson, combined with a powerful ex-rugby union back row of French, Warlow and Mantle to steamroller the opposition with deadly efficiency!

Yet it was the capture of Tommy Bishop from Barrow for £5,500 that completed the team-building jigsaw. The arrival of the 26 year old 'Mighty Atom' scrum half caused some controversy regarding Alex Murphy's position in the team. Peter Harvey was established as stand off and with Welsh half back Bob Prosser also available, Coan had no hesitation in asking Murphy to turn out in the centre-with Vollenhoven outside him! Although unhappy in his new role, the Skipper did a fine job alongside his co-centre 21 years old Billy Benyon-the 'Babe' of the team. *"A lot of rubbish was talked about what was best for the team,"* explains Coan. *"Murphy was the best player we had in any position-the greatest player you will ever see in your lifetime. Of course there was Tom Van Vollenhoven-but he was more of a specialist. Alex was the complete footballer, a fine athlete and a tremendous trainer."*

WEMBLEY - HERE WE COME!

St.Helens faced Wakefield Trinity at Belle Vue in the first round of the Challenge Cup, having suffered a 12-20 reversal seven days before. Yet the Super Saints secured a memorable 10-0 success, courtesy of a try by 'new boy' Bishop and Vollenhoven. *"Tom could still produce something extra just when we needed it,"* recalls Ray French. *"Although I think this was his only try during the cup run - it was certainly a vital one!"* Swinton fell at Knowsley Road in round two, before a controversial try by Alex Murphy floored Hull K. R. on the way to the semi-finals. An injured Vollenhoven sat out the 'Roses' clash against Dewsbury at Station Road, Swinton and watched Len Killeen pull the Saints out of a potentially embarassing situation with two brilliant opportunist tries and three goals in an uneasy 12-5 success.

St.Helens were to meet Wigan at Wembley in a repeat of the 1961 'Clash of the Titans.' Yet Wigan, the cup holders, were an ageing side, whose best moments had come twelve months before in a classic encounter with Hunslet. It was little wonder that the Saints left their Southport base for London in buoyant mood, physically refreshed and with a distinct psychological advantage. Wigan hooker Colin Clarke was forced to miss the final as a result of suspension. His replacement, Tom Woosey was essentially a prop forward and could not match the experience of his formidable opponent Bill Sayer-sold to St.Helens from Wigan before the cup deadline!

Injuries sustained in the play-off match with Hull K.R. robbed the St.Helens squad of Prosser and Coslett. Coan stuck with the side which had defeated Dewsbury, with Tom Van Vollenhoven replacing Tony Barrow on the right flank, the latter named as substitute, together with local lad Geoff Hitchen. *"Although I came in for the final,"* recalls Tom, *"At one stage it looked as though I wouldn't make it-the hamstring still wasn't right."* In fact, Vollenhoven was troubled with such injuries throughout his career, as former team-mate Ray French explains: *"I always say, jokingly, that Tom 'invented' the hamstring injury-which of course, is such a common injury in the modern game. I remember he pulled one just after I joined the Saints in the early 1960s. Coming from Rugby Union I was rather bewildered. If you had a sore leg-you gave it a rub and that was that! In reality, of course, it is a nasty injury. The original treatment of the injury....rest.....was wrong. Apparently a 'crusting-up' can occur in the leg. Nowadays, you are encouraged to maintain movement. I actually had one later in my career-six weeks of total frustration-like having a piece of elastic in your leg. You were always worried about it going again."*

ALL SAINTS DAY!

The 1965/66 season truly belonged to Len Killeen and it was no surprise when he booted over a 4th. minute penalty to edge the Saints ahead at Wembley. Yet Killeen went on to astound the 98,536 crowd-and millions watching on television-by hammering a second penalty kick over sixty yards to the target! In the 17th.minute, Saints' prop Albert Halsall stormed through a gaping hole in the Wigan defence and his pass was picked up by Harvey, who initially headed for the corner, before working a clever scissors movement with Vollenhoven. Just as he was tackled, Tom expertly released the ball to the supporting Mantle, who careered out of two attempted tackles to dive over for the crucial first try. Killeen's conversion gave the Saints a vital 9-0 lead. A Gilfedder penalty reduced the deficit to seven points before the interval.

The chant of 'Easy.....Easy....' rang out from the jubilant St.Helens supporters in the 54th. minute as Benyon's tantalising grubber kick was picked up by his winger Killeen, who dived full length to gather the ball cleanly and place it

Threshold of Glory 1965-66

St.Helens line up in their 'derby day blue' jerseys before the 17-10 success over the 'Old Enemy' Wigan on April 8th.1966. Vollenhoven, Murphy and Tony Barrow were the try-scorers. Len Killeen (3) and Alex Murphy kicked the goals in front of nearly 35,000 spectators! A Wembley and Championship 'double' was just around the corner!
Back Row L to R: TOM VAN VOLLENHOVEN, right wing. Recovered from career-threatening knee injuries of the previous season. Still a force to be reckoned with. RAY FRENCH, second row. Strong-running, hard-tackling 'Pack Leader,' now a leading television personality. CLIFF WATSON, prop-forward. Most powerful number ten in world rugby. Automatic choice for the Australasian tour at the end of the 1965/66 season. Now resident Down Under. JOHN WARLOW, second row. Ex-Llanelli Rugby Union forward. An international in both codes of rugby. FRANK WARD, prop forward. Local lad filling in for the injured Albert Halsall. BILL SAYER, hooker. Great Britain international, bought from Wigan before the transfer deadline for a bargain fee. Faced 'hookerless' former club several months later at Wembley! JOHN MANTLE, loose forward. All-round athlete. Ex-Newport Rugby Union forward-arguably the finest forward ever to come out of Wales. BRIAN HOGAN, substitute forward. Note the distinctive hairstyle! St.Helens-born and a future international who found fame with Wigan, Workington, Widnes and Bradford.
Front Row L to R: PETER HARVEY, stand off. Ex-Liverpool R.U.F.C. Scottish-born, later transferred to Warrington. BILLY BENYON, left centre. 'Babe' of the team. Had trials with Bolton and W.B.A. before turning to Rugby League. County and international centre, who made a staggering 510 appearances for St.Helens, from 1961-77. TOMMY BISHOP, scrum half. The 'Mighty Atom.' Local lad signed for £5,500 from Barrow before the cup deadline in 1966. Toured Australia in same year, where he now lives. ALEX MURPHY, right centre. Went on to become the only St.Helens-born player to lift the Challenge Cup with the Saints at the end of the campaign. Note padding on right upper arm-a legacy of a serious injury from the Australian Tour of 1962. FRANK BARROW, full back. Former Saints' junior. Fearless running and tackling made him a big crowd favourite at Knowsley Road. County representative. LEN KILLEEN, left wing. Kicked longest-ever goal at Wembley in the 1966 Challenge Cup Final. Appeared in a Grand Final for Australian club Balmain in 1969. TONY BARROW, substitute back. Utility player who went on to partner Tom Van Vollenhoven in the centre in the late 1960s. Transferred to Leigh, winning a Challenge Cup Winner's medal in 1971.

over the line virtually in one glorious movement. At 14-2, leg-weary Wigan were a beaten side. As the match entered it's final quarter, Tommy Bishop grubbered his way through for another touchdown close to the line. Killeen's conversion was a formality as the inevitable strains of 'Ee-aye-addio....we've won the Cup!' filled the Stadium. Alex Murphy's dropped goal two minutes from time merely rubbed salt into the wounds. At 21-2 the younger, fitter Saints had inflicted the biggest-ever Challenge Cup Final defeat on their arch rivals, a magnificent team performance and the second time in five years that Wigan had failed to score a try against St.Helens at Wembley!
Yet midway throught the second half Tom Van Vollenhoven had brought the crowd to it's feet with a typical piece of skill. Just when he appeared to be hemmed in at the corner by a posse of defenders, a little jink inside left Gilfedder for dead as he surged for the line, despite full-back Ashby's last-ditch tackle. *"The referee gave the try, originally, but the touch judge ruled that I was in touch,"* recalls Tom ruefully. Although the great man did not figure on the scoresheet, his successful marking job on Trevor Lake made a vital contribution towards the team's ultimate victory!

After Skipper Murphy had received the trophy from Prime Minister Harold Wilson came the news of Len Killeen's award of the Lance Todd Trophy as Player of the Match. Len and Alex were later interviewed by the B.B.C.s David Coleman. *"We're going to paint the town red tonight,"* promised Murphy, *"And we'll go home on Monday night to the biggest reception ever known"* .....*"And then win next Saturday and win the Double,"* chirped a confident Killeen.

Although Tom enjoyed those fantastic scenes that his Captain had promised back in St.Helens, he was not fit enough to play in the Championship Final against Halifax seven days later. Tony Barrow replaced him on the right wing as the Saints went on to crush the Yorkshiremen by 35-12 and achieve a memorable double triumph! It was a proud moment for every St.Helens fan as Alex Murphy held the Championship trophy aloft to signify the club's magnificent four-trophy haul and a place amongst the immortals of Rugby League. The Super Saints had made a significant contribution to a fabulous year of sport in 1966, including England's World Cup Final success over West Germany at Wembley....the Cooper-Ali fight and, nearer home, Everton's F.A. Cup Final victory over Sheffield Wednesday and Liverpool's League Championship triumph. Halcyon days indeed!

CHALLENGE CUP FINAL
ST.HELENS 21 WIGAN 2
AT WEMBLEY STADIUM
SATURDAY 21st.MAY 1966

ST.HELENS F.Barrow; Van Vollenhoven, Murphy (Capt. goal), Benyon, Killeen (5 goals, try); Harvey, Bishop (try); Halsall, Sayer, Watson, French, Warlow, Mantle (try). Subs.A.Barrow, G.Hitchen

WIGAN Ashby; Boston, D.Stephens, Ashton (Capt.), Lake; C.Hill, Parr; Gardiner, Woosey, Mc.Tigue, T.Stephens, Gilfedder (1 goal), Major. Subs.Hesketh, Lyon

Referee-Hunt (Warrington)
Attendance-98,536
Receipts- £50,409 (Record)
Lance Todd Trophy-Killeen (St.Helens).

Now for the double!
Saints' skipper Alex Murphy holds the Challenge Cup aloft after the 21-2 demolition of Wigan in 1966. Other St.Helens players are (left to right) Albert Halsall, Cliff Watson, Tommy Bishop, Frank Barrow, Bill Sayer, John Warlow, Len Killeen, Billy Benyon, Tom Van Vollenhoven and Peter Harvey.

CHAPTER TEN

The last waltz

AFTER THE LORD MAYOR'S SHOW!

When the St.Helens squad lined up for the cameraman before the start of the 1966/67 season-complete with four gleaming pieces of silverware-there was one noteable absentee. Despite being the most successful captain in Saints' history, Alex Murphy was unhappy at being 'shifted out' to the threequarters and told the club that he had no intention of playing out of position in the centre again-even with the great Tom Van Vollenhoven outside him! Indeed, the Championship Final against Halifax proved to be Murphy's last game in a St.Helens jersey. After being transfer-listed at £12,000 and linked with Australian club North Sydney, Murphy shocked the Rugby League world by joining Leigh as Coach. Since he had no intention of playing for the East Lancashire club, the perplexed St.Helens Board would receive no compensation whatsoever! The famous 'Four Cups' side had started to break up even before the new season had got under way!

A final flourish!
Proud skipper Vollenhoven with the Lancashire Cup after the defeat of Warrington in 1967.
(St.Helens Reporter)

The game itself was to change in character during the new campaign. The scrum which followed a penalty kick to touch was abolished and replaced by a tap-kick at the point of entry. To prevent teams from keeping the ball for long spells during a match, a scrum was to be formed after four consecutive tackles, unless the attacking side had kicked or otherwise given away possession. Yet rule changes apart, the club found the task of following the four cups success a daunting prospect. The loss of Murphy-Skipper and Master Tactician-was a severe blow. Injuries and loss of form further upset the rhythm of the side-especially in the cup competitions. Wigan triumphed at Central Park in round two of the Lancashire Cup and Saints surrendered their hold on the Challenge Cup after a shock 3-8 home defeat by Salford in a first round replay. St.Helens finished fourth in the league table behind the Yorkshire triumvirate of Leeds, Hull K.R. and Wakefield, yet still had cause for celebration by retaining the Lancashire League title for the third successive season.

Tom Van Vollenhoven played in 39 matches during the campaign and ran in 27 tries-his best performance since 1962/63. For the majority of those matches, especially in the first half of the season, his centre partner was Tony Barrow-who is in no doubt whatsoever about the capabilities of the man outside him at that time: *"Tom was simply the best-ever! He had the lot...speed, agility and he was big on defence ...the ability to ride a tackle and tremendous balance-especially when he side-stepped. It was a dream come true to play with him. When you made a half-break and gave him the ball he scored nine times out of ten. His positional sense was fantastic. You seemed to know instinctively when to give the ball to him. Another thing...if you backed up he would give it to you. He knew exactly when to come inside and would never move off his wing unless he was completely hemmed in. Some would come off their wing too early-not Tom-he was dynamite! Trouble is...I played with other wingers and expected more from them! He was not a flashy fellow, he would just do the business quietly and efficiently. After the match he was never quite the life and soul of the party-but he would always have a laugh. He liked a drink and smoked-quite surprising that his speed was not affected. Mind you, I remember watching him on the training ground earlier in my career, with Murphy and Large. Murphy would scorch ahead for the first 10-20 yards; then Ken over 30 yards; after that Vol. would simply kill 'em for pace!"*

The Saints played their best football towards the end of the 1966/67 campaign by trouncing Alex Murphy's Leigh 37-12 in the first round of the Championship Play Offs. Victories over Castleford and Bradford put them into the final against Wakefield Trinity at rain-lashed Headingley on May 6th. Although Joe Coan's men came away with a creditable 7-7 draw, it was a different story four days later at Swinton. A 33,537 crowd saw Trinity hit top form against a jaded-looking St.Helens side to win by 21-9, despite Vollenhoven's try that kept the Saints in the hunt in the first half.

LEAGUE CHAMPIONSHIP FINAL (REPLAY)
ST.HELENS 9 WAKEFIELD 21
AT STATION ROAD, SWINTON
WEDNESDAY 10TH.MAY 1967

ST.HELENS F.Barrow, Van Vollenhoven (Capt. try), A.Barrow, Smith, Killeen (2 goals); Douglas, Bishop (1 goal); Warlow, Sayer, Watson, French, Hogan, Mantle.

WAKEFIELD TRINITY Cooper; Hirst (try), Brooke (2 tries), N.Fox (3 goals), Coetzer; Poynton (Capt. try), Owen (try); Bath, Prior, Campbell, Clarkson, Haigh, D.Fox.

Referee-Manley (Warrington)
Attendance-33,537
Receipts- £9,800
Harry Sunderland Trophy-Owen (Wakefield)

At thirty-three years of age and with almost ten full seasons of rugby league behind him, Tom declared his intentions of retiring from the game and returning home to South Africa at the end of the following campaign. He was duly appointed Team Captain for 1967/68 - he had skippered the side, in fact, during the latter stages of the previous season - and granted a testimonial in recognition of his ten years service to the St.Helens club.

THE CALYPSO KING!

A hard-working Testimonial Committee organised fund-raising events on Tom's behalf throughout St.Helens. The club published a special edition of it's Yearbook for 1967/68 including a special tribute to the 'Flying Springbok,' written by Secretary Basil Lowe. Yet one of the most innovative mementoes of Tom's ten year career at St.Helens was the production of a special commemorative record entitled 'The Vollenhoven Calypso.' Les Charnock, with his connections in the music business, helped to organise the project: *"Initially, we ran a competition in the St.Helens Reporter for suitable lyrics, which we put to a catchy calypso beat. The song was recorded at the Chart Studios in Liverpool, with a fellow called Reggie Byron on lead vocal. On the flip side we recorded spoken tributes from some of Tom's former team-mates.....Alan Prescott, Alex Murphy, Duggie Greenall and Vince Karalius...with Basil Lowe doing the introductions. The whole thing was very much a novelty-especially as far as rugby league was concerned and is quite a collector's item to day!"*

A CAPTAINS PART!

As Skipper, Tom Van Vollenhoven witnessed the end of an era during his final season at Knowsley Road. The break-up of the 1966 Wembley team continued with the loss of Len Killeen to Australian club Balmain at the end of the 1966/67 campaign.

"Len was a great points scorer and a very flamboyant footballer," remembers Tom. *"He would score tries by kicking over the full-back and catching it...or from interceptions. I tended to play safe in defence and would rarely go for the interception. I would normally stay with my opposite number ready to put the tackle in."* Indeed, Len picked up a Grand Final Winner's Medal with Balmain in 1969-one of a select band of players who have achieved a Grand Final and Wembley 'double' success!

The break-up continued with the transfer of Ray French-who had skippered the Saints through the difficult period following the four cups success-to Widnes and Peter Harvey to Warrington. Peter recalls a conversation with one of his new team-mates, full-back Keith Affleck before a match against St.Helens: *"Keith asks me about Vollenhoven ....'Which way will he go?' I said that he would go any way he likes. 'Which way does he favour?' I replied that which ever way he would send you he would go in the opposite direction! Anyhow, we went out and Vol. broke through on his own with only the full-back to beat. Keith never touched him. Tom sent him on the outside, beat him on the inside and went under the posts. 'You're right....you don't know where you are with him,' Keith admitted to me after the match!"*

The team enjoyed success in the early rounds of the Lancashire Cup before reaching the Final against Warrington at Central Park, Wigan, on October 7th., 1967. Tom's first major final as captain did not go according to plan, however, as a disappointing game ended all-square at 2-2. When the replay took place at Swinton on December 2nd.-nearly two months later-spectator interest had waned considerably. The threat of fog and live television coverage

Saints in transition 1967-68

St.Helens line up for the camera before the 10-2 League victory over Oldham at Knowsley Road on Saturday, November 16th.1967. Skipper Vollenhoven and his centre, Billy Benyon scored tries. Coslett and substitute John Houghton kicked a goal apiece. Notice the temporary scaffolding which supported extra lighting required for colour transmission of matches in the B.B.C.2 Floodlit Trophy Competition.
Back Row L to R: DON STILLWELL, substitute forward. Local lad, whose career was halted by a broken arm. A design engineer currently working in the U.S.A. FRANK MYLER, left centre. Ex-Widnes Wembley winner in 1964. Captain of the 1970 Great Britain Australian touring squad. JOE ROBINSON, second row. Local product from the U.G.B. club. Finished career with Barrow. KEL COSLETT, loose forward. Former full back who switched to the number 13 jersey with great success. Kicked 1,698 goals for St.Helens during his career. JOHN WARLOW, prop forward. Hard, uncompromising Welshman, who made 4 appearances for Great Britain before joining Widnes in the early 1970s. ERIC CHISNALL, second row. Superb, home-grown running back-rower. One of three brothers to play professional rugby. County and international forward. JOE EGAN, hooker. Son of one of Wigan's all-time greats-a hooker himself-Joe Egan Snr. Later joined Blackpool Borough. BRIAN HOGAN, prop forward. 'Man of the match' against Oldham. Transferred to Wigan in December 1968. JOHN HOUGHTON, substitute back. Former Blackbrook amateur star. Utility back and goalkicker, later joined Swinton. Now sadly deceased.
Front Row L to R: FRANK BARROW, full back. Made position his own when Coslett broke an ankle in 1964/65. Made over 200 appearances for the Saints. BILLY BENYON, right centre. Local lad, signed at 16, who went on to play in 20 major finals for St.Helens from 1962-77. TOM VAN VOLLENHOVEN, right wing. Vastly experienced and a natural choice as captain. In the middle of a very successful Testimonial Year. TOMMY BISHOP, scrum half. Skipper of Club, County and Country in 1968/69. Later led Australian club Cronulla to a Grand Final appearance in 1973. LES JONES, left wing. Signed from local amateur rugby in February 1967. Scored on his first team debut against Wigan at Central Park. County and Great Britain representative. GARTH ROBERTSON, stand off. Rhodesian, who trialled for Wigan under the name of Southey. 10 full appearances during the season-one as centre to Vollenhoven-before returning home to play rugby union once more!

reduced the crowd to just 7,500 hardy souls-less than half the previous total. *"Only die-hards travel these days,"* wrote a rueful Tom Ashcroft, *"When there is a cheap and easy television alternative at home!"*

The Saints won a closely-fought contest by 13 points to 10, with tries from youngster Les Jones-who was later to succeed Vollenhoven on the right flank-John Warlow and Eric Chisnall. Former Blackbrook amateur John Houghton kicked two goals. It was a proud moment for Tom Van Vollenhoven in his testimonial year as he lifted a trophy for the first time as Skipper of the side. Yet five weeks before, Tom had found that the Captain's lot was not necessarily a happy one. During the 8-4 victory against Australia at Knowsley Road - a real bad tempered affair - Tom had tried to break up a ding-dong scrap between Kangaroo scrum half Billy Smith and Saints' full-back Frankie Barrow. *"All of a sudden, Smith decided to take a swing at me,"* recalls Tom. *"The next thing I remember I was in Jim Murray' s dental surgery. Two teeth had been knocked out and I had to have several stitches for my trouble! Definitely one of the worst experiences of my career!"*

LANCASHIRE CUP FINAL (REPLAY)
ST.HELENS 13 WARRINGTON 10
AT STATION ROAD, SWINTON.
SATURDAY, 2ND.DECEMBER 1967

ST.HELENS F.Barrow; Vollenhoven (Capt.), Smith, Benyon, Jones (try); Douglas (sub. Houghton 2 goals), Bishop; Warlow (try), Sayer, Watson, Chisnall (try), Mantle, Coslett.

WARRINGTON Conroy; Coupe, Melling (try), Allen (2 goals), Glover; Scahill, Gordon (try); Ashcroft, Harrison, Price, Briggs, Parr, Clarke.

Referee-Lindop (Wakefield)
Attendance-7,500

A FINAL FLOURISH

Apart from county cup success and victory over Australia, the 1967/68 season brought disappointment with a shock 5-0 home defeat against Huddersfield in the first round of the Challenge Cup. Yet over £25,000 was spent on new players, including Widnes ace half-back Frank Myler, Aberavon's Welsh Rugby Union international forward Bobby Wanbon, Graham Rees and Austin Rhodes from Swinton, Mike Mc.Neil from Lancashire rugby union and John Walsh from the junior ranks. In January 1968, Coach Joe Coan resigned-not from bad results-but from criticism of the team's style of play, where too much emphasis had been placed on forward power. *"Once you establish a routine of winning, then comes the manner of the win,"* remembers Coan. *"You have to win with flair. You win one match by thirty points, then it's got to be forty-there's no end to it!"* Coan was succeeded by Welshman Cliff Evans, who had coached the great Swinton side of the early 1960s.

One particularly memorable moment for Tom Van Vollenhoven and Saints' new Coach came with the 24-13 home success against deadly rivals Wigan on Good Friday. It was a particularly poignant moment for Tom, making his final league appearance at Knowsley Road. Yet his old adversary Billy Boston was also playing in his last derby clash before retiring at the end of the season. Over 17,000 spectators - many with a whole host of memories of the two greats in their 'pomp'-saw the Flying Springbok grab the headlines in spectacular fashion with a well-taken hat-trick of tries to earn the 'Man of the Match' award. Three days later, Tom was to score his last try for the club in the 19-16 league success at Swinton-his 23rd. of the season.

THE LAST FAREWELL

One of the most emotional occasions ever witnessed at Knowsley Road occurred on April 24th.1968, when Tom Van Vollenhoven bade farewell to the scene of his many triumphs by leading the Saints to a 20-0 victory over Warrington in the second round of the Championship Play-Offs. Tom's superb all-round display earned him the Player of the Match Award, yet he was denied the opportunity of scoring the try some 16,000 spectators wanted from him, when referee Hunt disallowed his 30 yard effort for stealing the ball-quite legitimately-in a one-to-one tackle! After the final whistle, as he was carried shoulder-high to the tunnel by his team-mates, he turned to give a final salute to the supporters who had so often cheered him home. They would never see his like again!

Unfortunately, Tom's hopes of finishing his career with a Championship Medal were dashed three days later as the Saints crashed 23-10 to Hull K.R. at the now demolished Craven Park. The 14,000 crowd was swelled by many travelling Saints' fans who had made the long journey to Hull-there was no M62 motorway in those days-to cheer on their team and pay homage to the Flying Springbok. After what was his 409th. and final appearance as a Saint, Tom led both teams from the field to a standing ovation from both sets of supporters.

Tom's great rival, Billy Boston, also 'retired' on the same day after the Riversiders' defeat against Wakefield at Belle Vue in the other semi-final. Although Boston made a brief comeback with Blackpool Borough some time later, Tom's break with Rugby League was to be complete. Like all truly great sportsmen, he finished at the top, with dignity. Yet before those boots were to be hung up for the last time there was another marvellous occasion for Tom Van Vollenhoven to savour, as former team-mate Ray French recalls: *"Tom is only one of two South Africans to play for Great Britain-Dave Barends of Bradford Northern is the other. As a Widnes player, I was selected for the Great Britain squad to travel to Australia for the 1968 World Cup competition. We had three practice matches before we left, against Halifax, Salford and Leeds. I remember that the Rugby League 'Supremo' Bill Fallowfield insisted that Tom played for Great Britain in our first match against Halifax to honour him for his services to the game. Neil Fox was his centre....and Tom roared in for a brilliant hat-trick of tries in his last game of rugby league football!"*

TOMMY VOL - LIVING LEGEND OF RUGBY LEAGUE!

Before returning to South Africa with his wife and family, Tom was presented with a cheque for £2,800-the biggest amount ever handed over to a player in his testimonial year. After making the presentation, Saints' Chairman Harry Cook paid tribute to *"The finest wingman who ever graced a rugby field.....he has given us his best-his wonderful attacking ability, his willingness to leave his wing to help out in-field and his wonderful sportsmanship on the field."* Club Secretary Basil Lowe summed up the career of South Africa's greatest 'convert' in his own succinct manner: *"Tom has adapted himself to the pressure footballing fame brings and he has been a credit to St.Helens R.L.F.C.....What a change has come over him! When we met him at London Airport, on*

Were you there?

Dateline Wednesday 24th April 1968

The last Waltz! Tom Van Vollenhoven is carried from the pitch by his St.Helens team-mates John Warlow (Left), Tommy Bishop and Kel Coslett after his final appearance at Knowsley Road, against Warrington. On an evening charge with emotion, almost 16,000 spectators saw the Saints crush the Wires by 20-0 in the first round of the 'Top 16' Play-offs.

It had been a decade since Tom Van Vollenhoven had made his debut at Knowsley Road-and times were certainly changing! Indeed, in an increasingly technological age-twelve months away from Man's first steps on the moon-advertisers urged potential customers to ask for a home demonstration of the new colour televisions. Luxury items seem ridiculously cheap by today's standards. Motorists could purchase a brand-new Hillman Minx at a staggering £733, while a luxurious three piece suite could be secured from Gilroy's of Church Street for the princely sum of 37 Guineas. Green Shield stamps were an added incentive to shoppers! In the world of popular music, jazz giant Louis Armstrong-'Satchmo'-topped the charts with 'What A Wonderful World.' Fellow American Bob Dylan had the best-selling long-player entitled 'John Wesley Harding.' Meanwhile at the Plaza Theatre Club in Duke Street, Joe 'Mr.Piano' Henderson was in residence. An exotic dancer was set to delight customers on a Thursday evening (Billed as a 'male treat'), while Surewin Bingo had replaced the flix at the Hippodrome. Disatisfaction with events in the wider world was revealed in a letter to the St.Helens Reporter, advocating that 'The people of Vietnam should decide their own future and that all foreign troops be withdrawn!

Fond farewells...
Here's to a living legend of Rugby League!
Saints' Chairman Harry Cook presents Tom with a record testimonial cheque for £2,800.
(St.Helens Reporter)
Behind every successful man!
A bouquet for Tom's wife Leonie.
(St.Helens Reporter)

Saturday 19th.October 1957, he was a bewildered and lost young man. He has since delighted thousands of supporters and millions of television viewers and brought artistry and real sportsmanship to the Rugby League game.....he will now become a living legend. His name will go down in history as one of the finest wingers-if not the finest-ever to play Rugby League football."

Peter Harvey is in no doubt as to Tom Van Vollenhoven's status among the all-time greats of sport: *"Tommy Vol. was a superstar....he drove a Mini Cooper 'S'....nobody else did! That's the difference. Vol. was the star. We all recognized him as a star. He was an artist. I asked Tom to try and teach me what he did. He looked at me rather puzzled and said 'I can't-because I don't analyse what I do. I just know when to do it.' That is artistry-pure and simple!"*

The perfect ambassador

Tom, wife Leonie and three children returned to South Africa for good in the Autumn of 1968. He took up a position with Pilkington Brothers in Springs-where he lives to this day-having worked for the parent company back in St.Helens. Sport is Tom's life and he clearly misses the camaraderie of the rugby dressing room: *"I suppose I have a relatively dull lifestyle...I am a sales rep. doing a lot of work around the mines,"* he reflects ruefully. He played hockey for a while, until an old knee injury forced him to retire. He also ran in mini-marathons, with a best time of 1 hour 40 minutes for 21 kilometres. He still manages to keep in excellent shape: *"I go to the gym several times a week and I play a bit of golf...especially at weekends."* Yet several years ago he suffered a detached retina. His vision is now limited to 80% and the surgeon attributed the injury to all the knocks he suffered-from the shoulders upwards-during his rugby career. *"We have a big garden and I like having barbecues...you know, that was one thing we found different when we first came to Britain...the houses seemed to be on top of each other!"* he remembers. *"We certainly have a lot more space where we live now...15 fruit trees...lawns both sides and back. It takes nearly two hours to cut them! My children are reasonably close ..daughter Lynn and my son-in-law are about half an hour's drive away in Johannesburg. Our youngest son is in Pretoria...but the other one, Keith jet-sets around everywhere."*

Indeed, Keith Van Vollenhoven...or Van Hoven as he is now known, has appeared in several major television commercials-including one for jeans with a New York backdrop, where he is 'frisked' by a

The perfect ambassador!
Tom signs autographs for youngsters on the Popular Side during a memorable lap of honour before the Ground Centenary Match against Australia.
(Brian Peers)

policewoman motorcyclist! He is a familiar face, certainly, although many people are unaware of the sporting link-even in St.Helens! Keith has also worked for the Gillette Company and once appeared on the B.B.C.s. prime time Terry Wogan Chat Show! He came back to England to live and was a fine 400 metre hurdler-and a member of the famous Haringay Club. It was Tom's old friend Les Charnock who suggested that he go into modelling....and he has never looked back since. He is currently pursuing a film career!

Tom and wife Leonie were flown to Britain as special guests of the Saints, who were celebrating the Centenary of their Knowsley Road Headquarters in September, 1990. Needless to say, Tom was the perfect choice as Figurehead for the celebrations, despite a somewhat frenetic timetable! *"Renewing old acquaintances-even with Duggie Greenall-has it's pitfalls and I will have to diet when I get home,"* he quipped. As well as attending countless social functions, the Vollenhoven's also enjoyed a short break in Ireland with Tom's old adversary Tony O'Reilly: *"I had not seen Tony since the 1955 Lions Tour until he came to South Africa for Dr.Craven's 80th.birthday celebrations in the Summer of 1990. Tony is very fond of the old chap and threw a party for him. That's the first time I have spoken to him since 1955! Cliff Morgan was there...Jeff Butterfield....and I just said in the conversation that I was going to St.Helens for the Centenary. He said that we must visit him in Ireland ...his Secretary made all the arrangements and we had a fabulous time!* "

An emotional re-union!
Former Chairman Harry Cook introduces Tom Van Vollenhoven to the Knowsley Road crowd before the Ground Centenary Match against Australia in 1990.
(Brian Peers)

Before the Centenary Match against the visiting Australians, the 15,000 crowd were treated to a parade of past Knowsley Road Greats. The reception given to Tom Van Vollenhoven was truly staggering and will remain with him for the rest of his life! Yet two days before Tom had been honoured by his induction into the St.Helens' Past Players Hall of Fame. The undoubted highlight of the evening was an interview by Tom's former colleague Ray French, which delighted the packed crowd in the Cabaret Room at Knowsley Road:

RAY FRENCH: *I first remember you came to prominence against the British Lions for the Springboks in 1955....*

TOM VOLLENHOVEN: *Yes, Ray. I had the privilege to play for South Africa against the British Lions in 1955 and I marked the famous Tony O'Reilly-now the Chairman of Heinz. Leonie and I have just spent three beautiful days in Ireland with him.*

RAY FRENCH: *It is said that you first heard of Rugby League from this fellow George Duckworth, the Baggageman with the M.C.C. cricket side out there?*

TOM VOLLENHOVEN: *In 1955 George Duckworth, who was then a Director at Warrington approached me to sign for them.*

RAY FRENCH: *Then Wigan and Saints entered the race.....*

TOM VOLLENHOVEN: *It was a tug of war-and we all know Harry Cook-he won the tug of war...and I'm pleased he won it!*

RAY FRENCH: *We have heard the story about the telegram boy carrying the message that Wigan would top any offer that St.Helens would make.......*

TOM VOLLENHOVEN: *I believe it's true. We had these telegram boys in South Africa at the time and he was actually on his way to our house and had a puncture. But Mr.Cook, with his foresight.......he had a Mercedes racing to the scene-it actually overtook the telegram boy!*

RAY FRENCH: *Your first impressions of this country?*

TOM VOLLENHOVEN: *Hectic! I didn't even have to go through customs. I don't know how the man does it...Cookie....before I knew it I was being whisked away to the television studios in Manchester to be interviewed by Eddie Waring. The next day we had a big press conference and Jim Sullivan pushed me into a corner...and answered every question they asked me!*

RAY FRENCH: *Your debut against Leeds....Ray Price made the break for you to score.....*

TOM VOLLENHOVEN: *That's correct....but before I scored, I let Pat Quinn in to score a try against me....and I can remember Alan Prescott coming over to me. The ball was over the try line-I was new to the game and did not know what to do. 'Precky' says...I won't mention the exact words...'Kick the ball over the stand, lad!' Yes....with Ray Price all I had to do was run it in!*

RAY FRENCH: *The Championship Final try against Hunslet, when you beat five men?*

TOM VOLLENHOVEN: *Ah yes! But you know I could never have scored that try without that pass from Duggie Greenall!*

RAY FRENCH: *You certainly were a fine combination.....*

TOM VOLLENHOVEN: *Yes...I did all the tackling!*

RAY FRENCH:*....And he did all the running?*

TOM VOLLENHOVEN: *He did all the talking!*

RAY FRENCH: *Any tries stand out?*

TOM VOLLENHOVEN: *All 392 of them were favourites! One try that stands out in my mind was against Warrington. I kicked over and Eric Fraser was waiting for the ball. I took the ball literally out of his hands and as I turned around he stood there and said 'I don't believe it!' It's tries like that I love!*

RAY FRENCH: *Did you want the ball early or did you prefer an overlap? When we played with you, it seemed as long as you got the ball you didn't mind......*

TOM VOLLENHOVEN: *I preferred an overlap! But a remark I heard the other night from our 'Happy Hooker' Bob Dagnall...he said when he got up from the scrum and saw my head go down on one side he used to say 'Stop running, lads...it's a try!'*

RAY FRENCH: *Were you conscious of your head going down on one side-especially in fifth gear?*

TOM VOLLENHOVEN: *No, Ray...I was never conscious of it!*

RAY FRENCH: *I spoke to you last Saturday before the Lancashire Cup Final-Widnes versus Salford - the first Rugby League match you had seen for a number of years. What did you think of it?*

TOM VOLLENHOVEN: *When I first came over we had the unlimited tackle rule, yet we scored a lot of tries in those days. I was surprised...I thought I might see more tries. I was disappointed really!*

RAY FRENCH: *........And Martin Offiah..........?*

TOM VOLLENHOVEN: *You can see he's got it. I like the way he backs away then moves around and goes. Yes...very impressive. He certainly has the speed!*

RAY FRENCH: *What do you think about the current political situation in South Africa and it's effect upon sport?*

TOM VOLLENHOVEN: *I have a lot of faith in President De Klerk and he reckons that South Africa will host the 1995 Rugby Union World Cup. If they have that optimism, then things are definitely looking up!*

RAY FRENCH: *Chatting to David Oxley, he tells me that the Rugby League have had overtures from people in South Africa to set up professional rugby over the past ten years. The Rugby League would not entertain them because of the the apartheid situation. Could it be an opportunity to expand?*

TOM VOLLENHOVEN: *Apparently there is too much money in South African Rugby Union. People are getting more money now than we got as professionals!*

RAY FRENCH: *........More than £14 for a win, Tom?*

TOM VOLLENHOVEN: *You better believe it! Put it this way, I'm glad I wasn't playing for Wigan in 1966 when they lost!*

Tom Van Vollenhoven in Rugby League, a complete record.

SEASON BY SEASON
APPEARANCES AND SCORING RECORD

	ST.HELENS			RUGBY LEAGUE XIII		
	APPS	TRIES	PTS	APPS	TRIES	PTS
1957-58	30	38	114	1	2	6
1958-59	44	62	186	1		
1959-60	42	54	162			
1960-61	45	59	177			
1961-62	38	45	135	2	1	3
1962-63	37	33	99			
1963-64	35	22	66			
1964-65	22	11	33			
1965-66	39	18	54			
1966-67	39	27	81			
1967-68	38	23	69			
TOTALS	409	392	1176	4	3	9

FIELDS OF BATTLE - ST. HELENS R.L.F.C.

		APPS	TRIES
Knowsley Road	(St.Helens)	206	240
Station Road	(Swinton)	17	11
Central Park	(Wigan)	15	5
Craven Park	(Barrow)	12	10
The Willows	(Salford)	12	8
Belle Vue	(Wakefield)	11	10
Naughton Park	(Widnes)	11	8
Borough Park	(Blackpool)	10	13
Athletic Grounds	(Rochdale)	10	10
Watersheddings	(Oldham)	10	5
Hilton Park	(Leigh)	9	8
Wilderspool	(Warrington)	9	7
Headingley	(Leeds)	9	3
Derwent Park	(Workington)	8	2
Knotty Ash	(Liverpool City)	7	13
Thrum Hall	(Halifax)	7	2
Recreation Ground	(Whitehaven)	7	2
Parkside	(Hunslet)	6	7
Post Office Road	(Featherstone)	6	5
Fartown	(Huddersfield)	5	7
Craven Park	(Hull K.R.)	5	1
The Boulevard	(Hull)	4	5
Wheldon Road	(Castleford)	4	2
Odsal Stadium	(Bradford)	2	4
Lawkholme Lane	(Keighley)	2	1
Empire Stadium	(Wembley)	2	1
Barley Mow	(Bramley)	1	1
Crown Flatt	(Dewsbury)	1	1
Mount Pleasant	(Batley)	1	0

Perfect partners!
Tom creates a try for his centre Cen Williams during the 40-5 league victory over Hull Kingston Rovers at Knowsley Road on Saturday 14th September 1963. The ex-Cardiff Rugby Union centre partnered Vollenhoven on 47 occasions - a number beaten only by Ken Large and Duggie Greenall.
(Rugby Leaguer)

FIELDS OF BATTLE
OTHER REPRESENTATIVE MATCHES
RUGBY LEAGUE XIII

		APPS	TRIES
Headingley	(Leeds)	1	2
Knowsley Road	(St.Helens)	1	0
White City	(Manchester)	1	0
Parc Des Princes	(Paris)	1	1

TRIES PER MATCH - ST.HELENS R.L.F.C.

Blackpool Borough	1.70
Liverpool City	1.47
Barrow	1.34
Whitehaven	1.33
Featherstone Rovers	1.30
Rochdale Hornets	1.29
Hunslet	1.20
Salford	1.19
Workington	1.11
Dewsbury	1.00
Keighley	1.00
New Zealand	1.00
Swinton	0.96
Halifax	0.92
Huddersfield	0.91
Wakefield Trinity	0.91
Hull	0.90
Widnes	0.80
Leigh	0.77
Warrington	0.64
Hull K.R.	0.61
Oldham	0.57
Leeds	0.56
Wigan	0.53
Batley	0.50
Bramley	0.50
Castleford	0.41
Australia	0.25

TRIES PER MATCH - RUGBY LEAGUE XIII

France	1.00
French XIII	1.00
New Zealand	0.00

CENTRE PARTNERS - ST.HELENS R.L.F.C.

1957-58	Greenall 24, Rhodes 4, Price 1, Forshaw 1.
1958-59	Greenall 37, Carlton 4, Smith 2, Howard 1.
1959-60	Large 26, Greenall 12, Landsberg 3, Rhodes 1.
1960-61	Large 29, Sullivan 5, Rhodes 3, Donovan 3, Briers 2, Landsberg 1, McGinn 1.
1961-62	Large 16, Briers 8, Northey 6, Sullivan 4, Huddart 3, Murphy 1.
1962-63	Briers 9, Williams 7, Sullivan 6, Donovan 5, McGinn 4, Smith 4, Northey 1.
1963-64	Williams 20, Northey 5, Killeen 2, Murphy 2, Todd 2, Davies 1.
1964-65	Williams 14, A. Barrow 3, Northey 4
1965-66	Murphy 14, Wood 13, Smith 7, Benyon 2, A. Barrow 2, Harvey 1.
1966-67	A. Barrow 31, Williams 3, Benyon 3, Douglas 2, Houghton 1.
1967-68	Benyon 21, Williams 3, Douglas 2, Whittle 2, A. Barrow 1, Smith 1, Blackwood 5, Robertson 1.

CENTRE PARTNERS - OVERALL TOTALS

Greenall	73
Large	71
Williams	47
A. Barrow	37
Benyon	26
Briers	19
Murphy	17
Northey	16
Sullivan	15
Smith	14
Wood	13
Donovan	8
Rhodes	8
Blackwood	5
McGinn	5
Carlton	4
Douglas	4
Landsberg	4
Huddart	3
Killeen	2
Todd	2
Whittle	2
Davies	1
Forshaw	1
Harvey	1
Houghton	1
Howard	1
Price	1
Roberston	1

CENTRE PARTNERS - RUGBY LEAGUE XIII

1957-58	Jones (Leeds) 1
1958-59	Greenall (St.Helens) 1
1961-62	Skene (Wakefield) 2

TOTAL APPEARANCES AND TRIES
ST.HELENS R.L.F.C.

OPPONENTS	APPS	TRIES
Barrow	23	31
Batley	2	1
Blackpool Borough	18	32
Bramley	2	1
Castleford	12	5
Dewsbury	3	3
Featherstone Rovers	10	13
Halifax	13	12
Huddersfield	12	11
Hull	10	9
Hull K.R.	13	8
Hunslet	10	12
Keighley	3	3
Leeds	16	9
Leigh	22	17
Liverpool City	17	25
Oldham	21	12
Rochdale Hornets	17	22
Salford	26	31
Swinton	27	26
Wakefield Trinity	23	21
Warrington	25	16
Whitehaven	15	20
Widnes	21	17
Wigan	26	14
Workington	17	19
Australia	4	1
New Zealand	1	1

TOTAL APPEARANCES AND TRIES
RUGBY LEAGUE XIII

OPPONENTS	APPS	TRIES
France	2	2
French XIII	1	1
New Zealand	1	0

Now you see him!
Tom about to beat Parker of Liverpool City in the league match at Knowsley Road on September 8th 1962. Teammate Ray French (far left) clearly does not relish the prospect of keeping up with the 'Flying Springbok' in full cry. Vollenhoven scored well over a try per match on average against the Green and Whites during his career. (St.Helens Reporter)

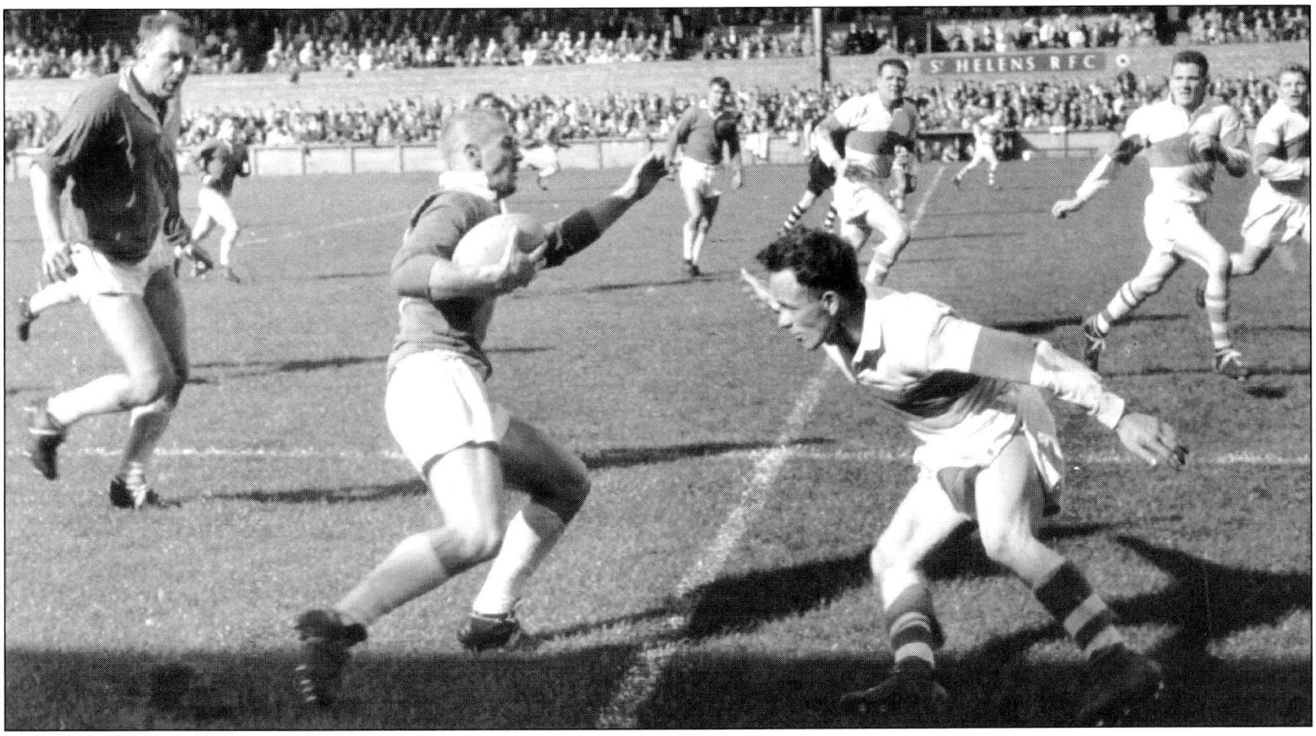

Ashton E.
'Glory In The Centre Spot' Pelham 1966

Chester R.H., Mc.Millan N.A.C.
'Men In Black' Pelham Books 1978

Fletcher R. Howes D (Eds.)
'Rothmans Rugby League Yearbook' (Various)

French R.
'My Kind Of Rugby' Faber 1979

Gate R.
'An Illustrated History Of Saints Versus Wigan Matches' Smiths (Wigan) 1990

Harvey, Charles (Editor).
'Sport International' Sampson, Low, Marston and Co. Ltd. 1960

Gaulton A.N.
'The Encyclopedia Of Rugby League Football' Hale 1968

Harvey C. (Ed.)
'Sports International' Sampson, Low, Marston and Co. Ltd. 1960

Hodgkinson D.
'Heroes Of Rugby League' Allen and Unwin 1983

Karalius V.
'Lucky 13' Stanley Paul 1964

Macklin K.
The Rugby League Game' Stanley Paul 1967

Macklin K.
The History Of Rugby League Football' (Rev.Edn.) Stanley Paul 1967

Morris G., Huxley J.
'Wembley Magic' Evans Bros. Ltd. 1983

Murphy A.
'Saints Hit Double Top' Pelham Books 1967

Open Rugby Magazine Number 56
'Van The Man' by P.Roberts

Parker A.C.
'Giants of South African Rugby' Howard Timmins, Cape Town, 1957.

Quinn K.
'The Encyclopedia Of World Rugby' Lochar 1991

Risman B. (Ed.)
'The Rugby League Football Book 2' Stanley Paul 1963

Roger, W.
'Old Heroes' Hodder and Stoughton 1991

Rugby League Record Keeper's Club-
Teams and Scorers booklets (Various)

Rugby Leaguer

St.Helens R.L.F.C. Handbooks (Various)

St.Helens Reporter

St.Helens Newspaper and Midweek Advertiser

St.Helens Star

Service A.
'The March Of The Saints' 1988

Waring E. (Ed.)
'The Eddie Waring Book Of Rugby League Football' Mueller 1966

Waring E.
'Rugby League-The Great Ones' Pelham Books 1969

Wigan Observer

Windsor's Rugby League Annuals-1962/63 1963/64